I0423773

STABILIZATION OF THE LOWRY RUINS

Adrian S. White and David A. Breternitz

Mesa Verde Research Center
University of Colorado
Boulder, Colorado

March 1976

FOREWARD

This presents the first of a series of cultural resource reports
in history and archeology on National Resource Lands in Colorado.

The intent of these publications is to make available to the public
and the professional community, cultural resource studies of the
Bureau of Land Management in Colorado.

Since its original excavation in the 1930's by Dr. Paul Martin, Lowry
Ruin had fallen into a serious state of disrepair. Public visitation
continued to increase. The need for stabilization became apparent.
Stabilization of the site, a National Historic Landmark, was under-
taken by contract with the University of Colorado beginning in 1966.
This work was completed by Ms. Adrian White, Dr. David Breternitz
and Al Lancaster of the University of Colorado.

Public distribution of a site specific stabilization report such as
this has not been done before. I feel the techniques and approaches
used at Lowry Ruin should be presented in their entirety as an example
of such work, and that the report should be made available to other
workers and the interested public. I encourage others in this field
to do the same.

It is satisfying to me to now be able to present the Lowry Ruin to
the visiting public in its repaired state. It is my hope that our
stabilization work, onsite interpretation and professional reports
regarding the sites, will result in a keener awareness by the public
of the importance of this non-renewable cultural resource.

DALE R. ANDRUS
State Director
Colorado
Bureau of Land Management

TABLE OF CONTENTS

Page

Abstract... ii

List of Figures.. iii

Organization of Report... viii

Introduction... 1

    Archaeology.. 4

    The Chaco Phenomenon... 7

Stabilization, 1974-75... 8

    History and Procedures... 8

    Kiva B, Temporary Roof... 20

    Kiva B and Room 27, 1975... 30

Stabilization Reports.. 44

    Walls.. 44

    Definitions.. 49

    Labor and Materials.. 49

    Ruins Stabilization Records.. 51

References Cited... 133

Appendix A - Correlation of Archaeological Features and
    Stabilization Reports.. 134

Appendix B - Tabulation of Labor and Materials, Stabilization
    Reports.. 136

Appendix C - Tabulation of Labor and Materials, by area....... 144

ABSTRACT

A record of past and recent stabilization activities at
Lowry Ruin is presented. Although initial excavation was
done in the 1930's, no formal ruin stabilization was
accomplished until 1966-67. In 1974-75 extensive maintenance stabilization was done, and the deeply buried, painted
kiva (Kiva B) was reexcavated, stabilized, and roofed for
public access.

Detailed records of activities in 1974-75 are presented,
and related to earlier work at Lowry Ruin. Recently
available tree-ring dates verify earliest building activity
began in A.D. 1090 for a period of 30 years. A relationship
of Lowry Ruin to the northern expansion of Chaco influence
in the late 1000's is suggested.

LIST OF FIGURES

Figure   Page

1. Lowry Pueblo and Great Kiva, topographic map 2

2. Lowry Pueblo, building sequence based on tree-ring dates.. 6

3. Lowry Pueblo, plan of Martin's excavations................ 9

4. Great Kiva, plan of Martin's excavations................. 10

5. Doorways stabilized by Ben Williford, 1936. a, Room 10,
   east doorway; b, Room 10, west doorway.................. 11

6. Room 9, north exterior wall, 1966. a, before
   stabilization; b, after stabilization................... 12

7. Lowry Pueblo, south end, 1966-67. a, before
   stabilization; b, after stabilization................... 13

8. Great Kiva, 1967. a, southeast view before
   stabilization; b, east view during stabilization........ 14

9. Great Kiva, 1967. a, room block to north during
   stabilization; b, drainage walls sloping outward........ 16

10. Lowry Pueblo, plan of Lancaster's stabilization, 1966-67.. 17

11. Great Kiva, plan of Lancaster's stabilization, 1966-67.... 18

12. Kivas A and B. a, area above Kivas before excavation,
    b, east side of Kiva B excavated to the floor........... 19

13. Wheelbarrow ramp. a, east-west profile; b, photograph,   21
    looking southwest, Kiva B in foreground.................

14. Kiva B. a, north view of murals; b, close-up of damage... 22

15. Kiva B, elevation of murals, Pilaster 1 to Pilaster 6..... 23

16. Kiva B. a, north-south profile of plastic sheeting over
    murals; b, north view of draped plastic................. 24

17. Kiva B. east-west profile of temporary roof............. 26

18. Kiva B, north-south profile of temporary roof........... 27

Figure   Page

19. Kiva B. a, north view of roof frame, temporary roof;
     b, north view of corrugated tin roof.................... 28

20. Rooms 31 and 27. a, Room 31, north view of beam steps;
     b, Room 27, entrance in north wall...................... 31

21. Wing wall connecting northwest exterior corner of Room
     27 and Kiva B. a, before construction; b, after
     construction.. 32

22. Kiva B, veneered doorway through southern recess.
     a, before construction; b, after construction.......... 33

23. Kiva B, entryway through southern recess. a, east-west
     profile of flagstone steps; b, east-west view after
     construction.. 34

24. Kiva B, rebar gate. a, front and side profiles; a, south
     view of gate.. 35

25. Kiva B, east-west profile of permanent roof............. 36

26. Kiva B, north-south profile of permanent roof.......... 37

27. Kiva B, permanent roof. a, north view of roof frame;
     b, north view of plywood roof and frame nailers........ 39

28. Kiva B, permanent roof. a, profile of plastic bubble; b,
     northeast view of plastic bubble secured to roof....... 40

29. Kiva B, permanent roof. A. North view of tarpaper layer
     and areas sealed with plastic cement; b, after
     addition of dirt layer................................. 42

30. Kiva B, drainage system. a, east-west profiles of
     drainage route; b, profile of drainage box............. 43

31. Room 27. a, south view of beams set in sockets over room;
     b, west view of plywood roof........................... 45

32. Lowry Pueblo, plan of CU stabilization, a, Lowry Pueblo; 46
     b, Kiva B.. 47

33. Great Kiva, plan of CU stabilization................... 48

Figures 34-73 accompany individual stabilization reports and show specific
work areas before and after stabilization; they are keyed to the numbered
stabilization reports.

iv

Figure		Report No.	Page
34a-b	Room 12, east exterior wall.................	1	52
35a-b	Room 14, east exterior wall.................	2	54
36a-b	Kiva E, south exterior wall.................	3	56
37	Kiva E, east exterior corner south of Kiva E	3	57
38a-b	Room 21, northwest interior corner..........	4	59
38c-d	Room 21, north interior wall................	4	60
39a-b	Room 11, west interior wall.................	5	62
40a-b	Great Kiva, stairway........................	6	64
40c	Great Kiva, stairway........................	6	65
41a-b	Great Kiva, northeast bench.................	6	66
42a-b	Great Kiva, east bench......................	6	67
43a-b	Great Kiva, west bench......................	6	68
44a-b	Room 16, south interior wall................	7	70
44c-d	Room 16, south interior wall................	7	71
45a-b	Room 14, south exterior entrance............	8	73
46a-b	Room 12, south exterior entrance............	9	75
47	Room 31, east interior wall.................	10	77
48	Room 8, east interior entrance..............	11	79
49a-b	Room 33, north end of west interior wall....	12	81
49c-d	Room 33, south end of west interior wall....	12	82
50a-b	Room 11, north exterior entrance............	13	84
51	Room 10, exterior entrance..................	13	85
52a-b	Room 27, north interior wall................	14	87
53a-b	Room 23, east exterior wall.................	15	89

Figure		Report No.	Page
54a-b	Room 23, north interior wall...............	15	90
55a-b	Space east of Kiva B (unnumbered), east interior wall............................	16	92
56a-b	Kiva B, northeast wall.....................	17	94
57	Room 24, south interior wall...............	18	96
58a-b	Room 21, east interior entrance...........	19	98
58c-d	Room 21, east interior entrance...........	19	99
59a-b	Room 4, southeast interior corner.........	20	101
60	Room 13, north exterior entrance..........	21	103
61	Kiva H, north interior wall...............	22	105
62a-b	Kiva B, pilaster 6........................	23	107
63a-b	Kiva B, pilaster 7........................	24	109
64a-b	Room 29, east interior wall...............	26	112
65a-b	Kiva B, pilaster 5........................	27	114
66	Kiva B, pilaster 4........................	28	116
67a-b	Kiva B, pilaster 3........................	30	119
68a-b	Kiva B, pilaster 1........................	31	121
69	Kiva B, pilaster 2........................	32	123
70	Kiva B, interior wall.....................	33	125
71a-b	Room 27, east exterior entrance...........	34	127
71c	Room 27, east exterior entrance...........	34	128
72	Kiva A, west wall.........................	35	130
73a-b	Room 31, north interior wall..............	36	132

ORGANIZATION OF REPORT

The Introduction gives the basic history of work at Lowry
Ruin, and presents new information regarding tree-ring
dates and the possible relationship with the so-called
Chaco Phenomenon.

History of Stabilization at Lowry Ruin gives an account
of the procedures followed and emphasizes the activities
involved with construction of the temporary and permanent
roofs, and the stabilization of Kiva B.

Stabilization Reports deal with walls, definitions of terms
utilized in descriptions, and labor and material tabulations
for each stabilization job.

The Ruins Stabilization Records are arranged in order of
the work. Each specific job is numbered sequentially and is
cross-referenced in Appendix A.

Appendix B is a tabulation of labor and materials by area
for work associated with Kiva B.

The Introduction is authored by Dr. David Breternitz. Ms.
Adrian White was responsible for field documentation; she
compiled the remainder of the report. Ms. Kellie Masterson
drafted the series of profiles of stabilization jobs.
Bertrand A. de Peyer produced the photographic plates and
Ms. Debbie Otterstrom typed the final manuscript.

INTRODUCTION

Lowry Pueblo is a well-known prehistoric ruin located nine miles west of Pleasant View and 28 miles northwest of Cortez, Colorado. It was initially excavated under the general direction of Paul S. Martin in 1930-31 and 1933-34 (Martin 1936, 1974) (Fig. 1). It is currently under the jurisdiction of the Bureau of Land Management (BLM) and on October 17, 1967 it was designated as a National Historic Landmark.

Between the time of initial excavation and National Landmark designation the BLM contracted with the University of Colorado to conduct stabilization activities under terms of BLM Contract No. 14-11-0008-0590-57. James A. Lancaster was in charge of the stabilization activities which took place in 1966-67. Mr. (Al) Lancaster had been a foreman for Dr. Martin during the 1930's work at Lowry. In the years between he had become the dean of the Mesa Verde archaeology and one of the founders of the art of ruin stabilization.

Since 1967, Lowry Ruin had been a local picnic area. Fortunately, it was decided in 1974 to develop the locality as a public facility. The impetus for subsequent activities came primarily from BLM personnel.

During the 1930's excavations, a unique painted kiva (Kiva B) was exposed, but safety and preservation dictated that this 17-foot-deep feature be refilled. The BLM wished to develop this particular kiva and additionally there were stabilization needs resulting from the lack of any ruin maintenance since 1967.

A set of circumstances enabled the development of a program of training, research, and interpretation from fall, 1974 through early summer, 1975. A project was established for the necessary maintenance stabilization of the ruin, reexcavation of the painted kiva, the training of graduate student archaeologists in ruin stabilization techniques under the direct supervision of Al Lancaster, and the development of a facility for the public that rivals anything currently available in the Four Corners region. A BLM (BLM Contract No. 52500-CT4-64(CN); University of Colorado Account No. 1705-52).

The eight-week field program was split into two 20-working-day sessions. As it worked out this procedure enabled us to conduct complex operations with a minimum of expense, and a maximum of efficiency.

A university course was established to provide academic credit for the graduate student participants (Anthropology 498/598). Because of circumstances beyond the control of the University and current hiring practices, Dr. David A. Breternitz was listed as both the Principal Investigator and as the instructor for the course. In actuality, Al Lancaster was in charge of the project in the field.

Figure 1. Lowry Pueblo and Great Kiva, topographic map.

The initial 20 days of field work began on August 21, 1974 and lasted through September 18. In addition to Breternitz and Lancaster, Larry V. Nordby served as Field Director. Participants were: three graduate students of the University of Colorado--E. Charles Adams, Curtis W. Martin, and Adrian S. White; two graduates from Fort Lewis College--James A. Head and L. Kent Leigy; one from Northern Arizona University--Jeffry Adams; one from the National Park Service--Neilson H. King; and David W. Kayer, who was with us for a week.

Between May 26 and June 17, 1975, another 20 days of field work were conducted. E. C. Adams, Head, Leidy, Martin, Nordby (released for the project through the courtesy of the Southwest Region, National Park Service), and White provided continuity in the field crew. In addition, we had Jenny L. Adams as cook and part-time stabilizer, Cory D. Breternitz (University of Arizona), and Leslie Nordby for part of the time.

This remarkable group of people performed tasks not heretofore done systematically by university students in the Southwest, or elsewhere as far as can be ascertained.

Many others were involved in the success of the project including all Bureau of Land Management people with whom we had dealings and who were most helpful. From the Denver Service Center, Lloyd Pierson and Roberto Costales saw the contract through; in the Colorado State Office, B. Gene Miller assisted at all levels; from the Montrose District Office, the District Manager, Marlyn Jones, supported the project from its inception, and Harry Lawson was most supportive and helpful.

Mr. Charles Brougher is the official custodian of Lowry Ruin. He provided help in many ways, including sharpening our tools. His wife's garden provided the team with "greens". Mr. John Pock built the grill-work gate in the painted kiva. He also fashioned special tools needed for stabilization and construction. Mr. Ken Stock is the only person in Montezuma County with facilities to cut a timber longer than 20 feet. He fashioned the timbers used to roof the painted kiva.

Mr. and Mrs. Roy Crow allowed us to use their farmhouse as headquarters during the fall 1974 session. In the spring of 1975 Darrel Lancaster allowed us to camp on his property in a barn built by Al Lancaster and utilize his water supply. For four weeks they made field life possible in a variety of adverse climatic conditions. Mr. Bill Head arranged for the use of the Montezuma County crane hoist to lift the huge timbers onto the walls on reconstructed Kiva B; he contributed a Sunday to operate the rig. The use of this hoist, donated by Mr. Curtis Honaker and the Board of County Commissioners for Montezuma County, is sincerely appreciated.

3

Archaeology

During Stabilization work in 1974-1975 little excavation resulting in
new materials was accomplished. Some 1100 potsherds were recovered
during the course of backdirt removal and in the process of stabilization excavations at the base of walls, etc. The sherds recovered do not
alter the picture presented by the original excavations by Martin.
Digging the trench for the drainage pipe, which extends from the roof
of Kiva B to the east of the ruin, two firepits were encountered; one
was in the northwest corner of Room 31, and other was 15m. east of the
outer wall of Room 31. Because of bulldozer work in this area in 1966,
there is no information regarding the depth of these features from the
original ground surface.

Martin (1936:204) did not have adequate chronological data to more than
suggest the period of occupation(s) of the Lowry Ruin. However, he does
discuss his interpretation of the architectural evidence and presents a
series of building periods (1936:194-202). The 1974-1975 work does not
alter his major conclusion that five major building periods took place,
even though we do have tree-ring evidence available for all of his
postulated construction stages.

At the present time there are a total of 34 tree-ring dates from Lowry
Ruin. Twenty-four of the dates are published in Robinson and Harrill
(1974:17-18):

Great Kiva			Room 19		
	GP-580	1064p - 1106v		FML-33-2	988p - 1085+rl
				FML-33-10	1000p - 1090+r
Kiva 1			Room 21		
	LOW-32	793 - 988vv		FML-33-15	1025 - 1089r
	LOW-31	960p - 1105vv			
Kiva A			Room 26		
	FML-33-3	987p - 1120rL		FML-33-14	887p - 1106cL
Kiva II or B			Room 27		
	LOW-27	1062p - 1106v		FML-33-1	792p - 1067vv
	LOW-26	1064p - 1106r		FML-33-2o	1041p - 1103rL
				FML-33-21	1061p - 1103rL
Room 8					
	LOW-33	799 - 1016vv	No Provenience		
	LOW-30	1063 - 1106r		FML-33-24	837p - 925+v
	LOW-28	977p - 1110r		FML-33-9	770 - 946+vv
				FML-33-13	868 - 1084vv
Room 11				LOW-34	1019 - 1089vv
	LOW-22	680p - 839vv			
	LOW-29	866 - 1120vv			
Room 15					
	LOW-21	781p - 989vv			
	LOW-25	1022 - 1088v			

The 1974 reexcavation of Kiva B produced additional dendro-samples which
have been dated (Robinson, personal communication, May 21, 1975).
Although these tree-ring dates are listed as being from both Kivas A and
B, the reexcavation of backdirt and the reuse of timbers in the construction of Kiva A tends to conclude that all ten of the dates are associated
with Kiva A. The tree-ring samples which were dates from the 1974
project are:

Kiva A				Kiva B			
LOW-41	719fp	–	985+vv	LOW-45	1060fp	–	1105vv
LOW-37	867+p	–	1027+vv	LOW-47	1069fp	–	1105vv
LOW-38	907+fp	–	1040++vv	LOW-46	987p	–	1109+v
LOW-39	957p	–	1053+vv				
LOW-40	967fp	–	1066vv				
LOW-42	911fp	–	1098+B				
LOW-36	898+p	–	1108++v				

Utilizing the presently available tree-ring evidence, a sequence of
construction can be suggested. Figure 2 diagrams an interpretation of the
present evidence, which indicates construction over a 30-year period,
beginning about 1090.

Period I is the construction of the four central rooms of Lowry which were
built in 1089-1090. This initial construction corresponds with Martin's
Earliest Stage, but does not include the Great Kiva, as proposed by Martin.

Period II is Martin's First Addition and the northern room block. There
are no tree-rings from rooms represented in this construction period.

Period III is the Second Addition of Martin, plus the construction of the
Great Kiva. The tree-ring evidence indicates that three rooms (26, 27, 8),
Kiva B and the Great Kiva were probably built between 1103 and 1110.
Architectural interpretation shows the block of rooms lying south of the
initial four-room block have common walls and bonds that indicate contemporary construction. However, with the available information, it is not
possible to pinpoint more accurately than in Figure 2. It is obvious that
certain contiguous rooms (to those with tree-ring dates) were also
constructed at this time: Rooms 20, 8, 6, 7, 17, 5,3, 4, 26, 27. Kiva B
was probably built in 1106.

Period IV is equivalent to Martin's Third Addition. In 1120 Kiva B was
remodeled into Kiva A.

There are no tree-ring dates for the peripheral rooms that lie on the
south and east margins of Lowry. These rooms are either contemporary with,
or somewhat later than, the construction of Kiva A.

In summary, construction undoubtedly took place over at least a 30-year
period, beginning about 1090. A postulated 50-year period of occupation
for Lowry Ruin still appears to be a reasonable estimate.

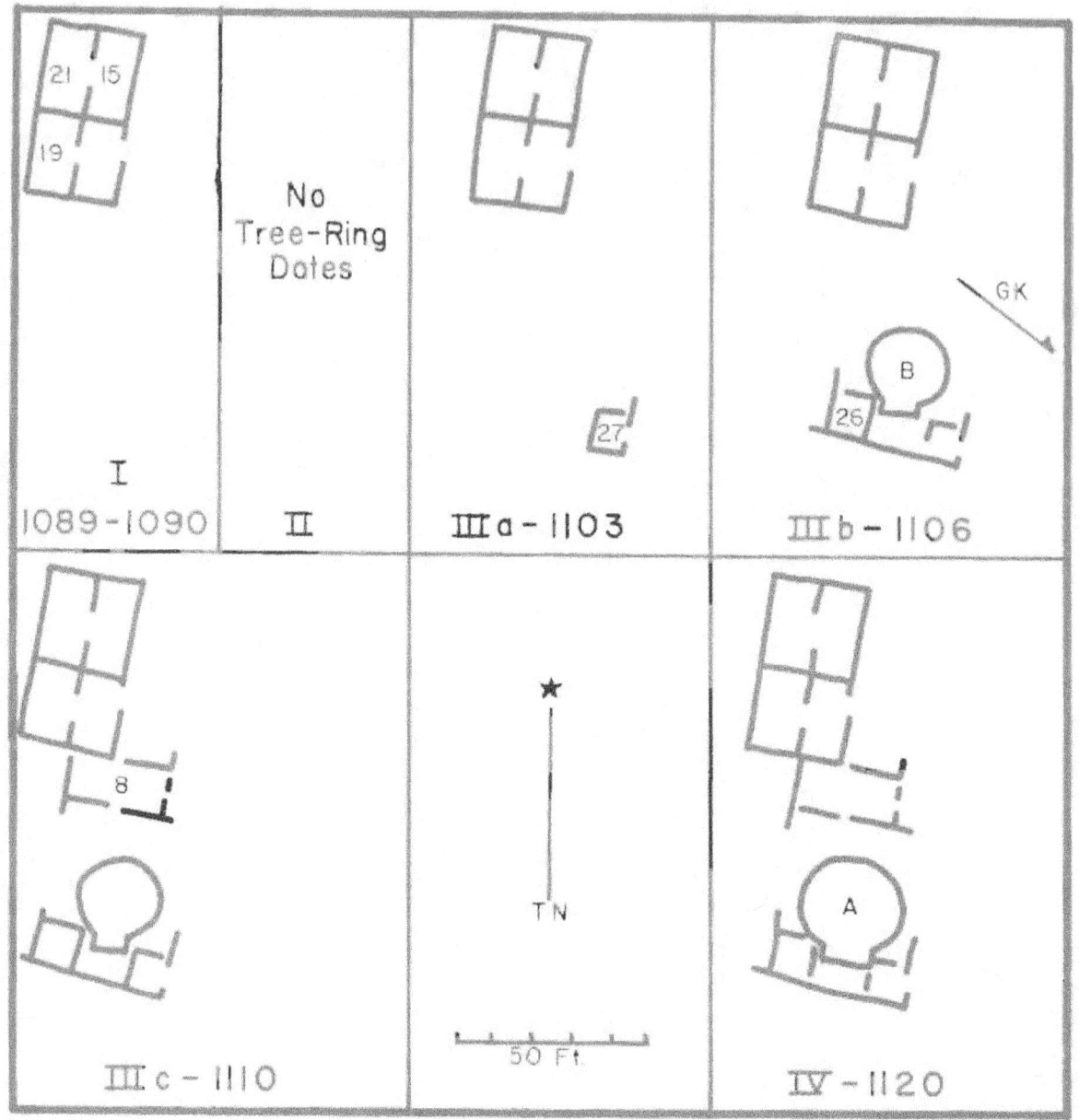

Figure 2. Lowry Pueblo, building sequence based on tree-ring dates. I, initial construction at 1089-1090; II, northern portion of ruin constructed but no tree-ring dates available; IIIa-c, construction between 1103 and 1110; IV, construction of Kiva A, over Kiva B, at 1120. Textual comments elaborate on the building sequence.

The Chaco Phenomenon

Robinson and Harrill (1974:18) note that the 1089-1090 construction at Lowry Ruin "...is remarkably consistent with other northern Chaco-like sites such as Aztec and the Salmon Ruin." In addition, the Chaco occupation of Chimney Rock Pueblo occurs at this time (Eddy 1972:24, 29, 59-63). Recent work at the Escalante Ruin, 2-3 miles west of the town of Dolores, has disclosed another northern, Chaco-style site that shows construction in the early years of the 1100's (Breternitz 1975:20; W. J. Robinson, personal communication).

The total ramification of the northern expansion of Chaco sites, which include site layout, architecture, and typical Chaco-like kivas, has yet to be fully explored. In the case of Lowry, with Chaco-like architectural features and the Great Kiva, it is simply pointed out that certain features at the site can be related to a larger cultural phenomonen that was wide-spread in the Mesa Verde Region at the end of the A.D. 1000's.

DiPeso (1974) has recently outlined the phenomena of the so-called "Puchteca" which involves resource gathering/trading stations which may be associated with the Mesoamerican-derived Chaco Development. Current and future research will help to clarify these relationships and explain the role of Lowry Ruin in the overall reconstruction of culture history for the Four Corners region.

History and Procedures

The stabilization of Lowry began in the thirties with original excavation under the supervision of Paul S. Martin (Figs. 3-4). Martin wanted to cap all the walls at Lowry but was unable to meet that expense. Ben Williford, who stabilized at Mesa Verde National Park, came to Lowry in 1936 and stabilized several small areas. He capped some walls in the southeast part of the ruin and a small area that separated Rooms 10 and 8. Two doorways and entrances to Room 10 were stabilized; they have received no additional work (Fig. 5). The joints were not pointed and the cement was allowed to remain to the front of the joint. This is interesting because it is indicative of early stabilization practices. It was thought to look more like prehistoric mortar. Two areas of Kiva B were protected and reconstructed before the area was backfilled. The roofing of the underground vent shaft was replaced. Murals covering the walls of the bench were coated with shellac to preserve them after the area was backfilled. When excavations were completed at Lowry some of the rooms were backfilled, as were Kivas A and B.

For the next 30 years no excavation or stabilization was done at Lowry. The elements caused rapid deterioration on the unsheltered ruin. Stones slipped from upper courses; prehistoric mortar crumbled; and lateral separation of walls occurred (Figs. 6-7). The Great Kiva eroded the most because it was constructed as a depression (Fig. 8).

In 1966 a joint Bureau of Land Management and University of Colorado effort began at Lowry to restore and stabilize the major above-ground features to preserve them for the public. Stabilization was begun at the southern end of the Pueblo. The major stabilization necessary is seen from before-and-after photographs taken of the north interior wall of Room 9 (Fig. 6) and from a view of the south end of the ruin (Fig. 7). Eighteen rooms and Kiva H were stabilized completely and six rooms were partially completed in the first season, which lasted three months.

The second season began in June, 1967. The Pueblo was completed and work began on the Great Kiva. The major reconstruction necessary to restore the Great Kiva is seen in Figure 8. Surface runoff down the walls and recessed stairway had caused rapid deterioration.

Lancaster used regular cement (Portland Type I and II) combined with Shiprock sand (sharp mortar sand) with calcium cloride added to slow down the curing process. Tamms mortar coloring, light buff, was added to the cement to reduce the blue-green cement color; this resulted in a light gray color. No new stone was quarried; old stone was reused from Martin's excavation; all cement was mixed by hand.

An account follows of the extensive restoration accomplished by Lancaster and his crew at Lowry Ruin in 1966-67. Wooden lintels were replaced in

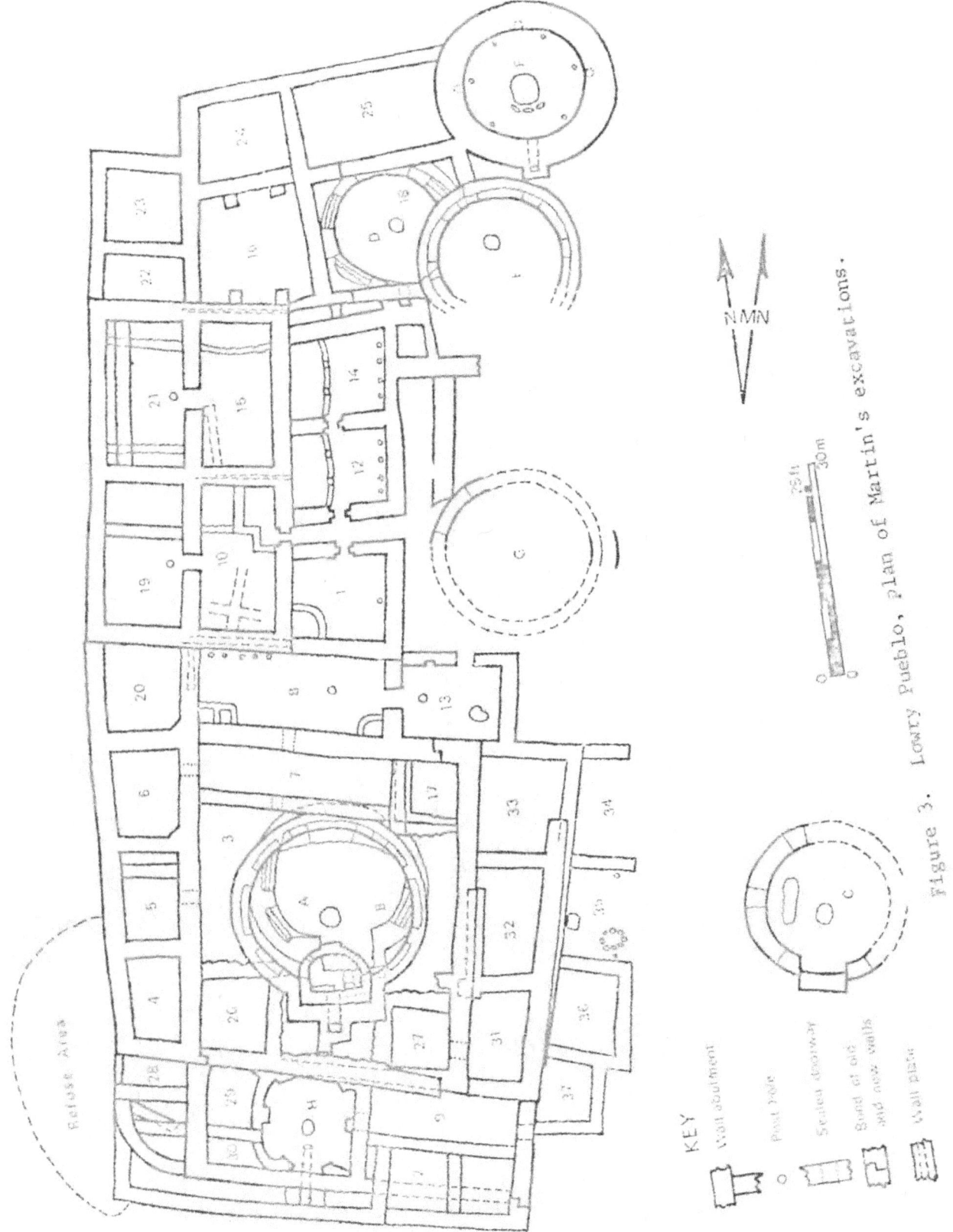

KEY

	Wall abutment
o	Post hole
	Sealed doorway
	Bond of old and new walls
	Wall plan

Figure 3. Lowry Pueblo, plan of Martin's excavations.

9

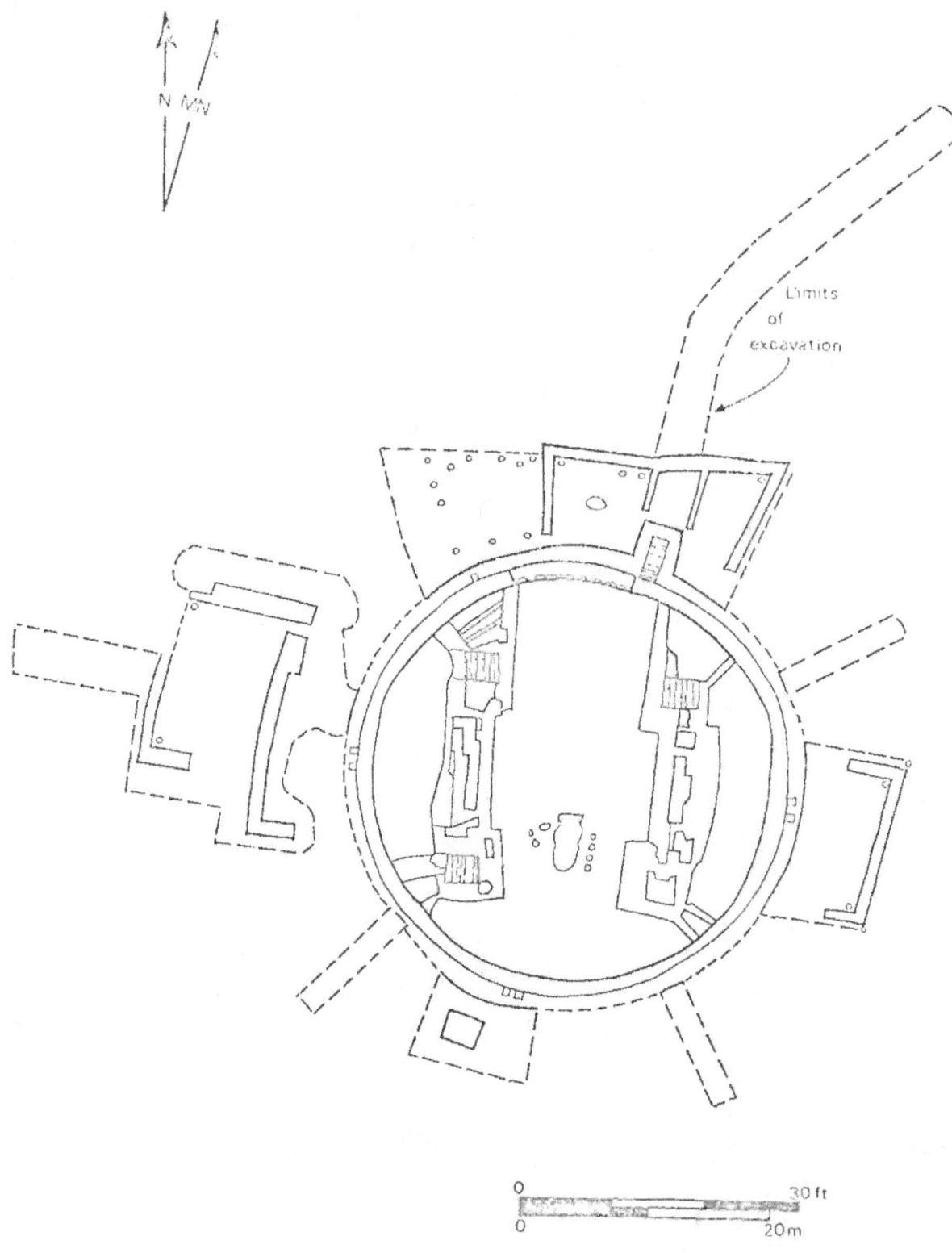

Figure 4. Great Kiva, plan of Martin's excavations.

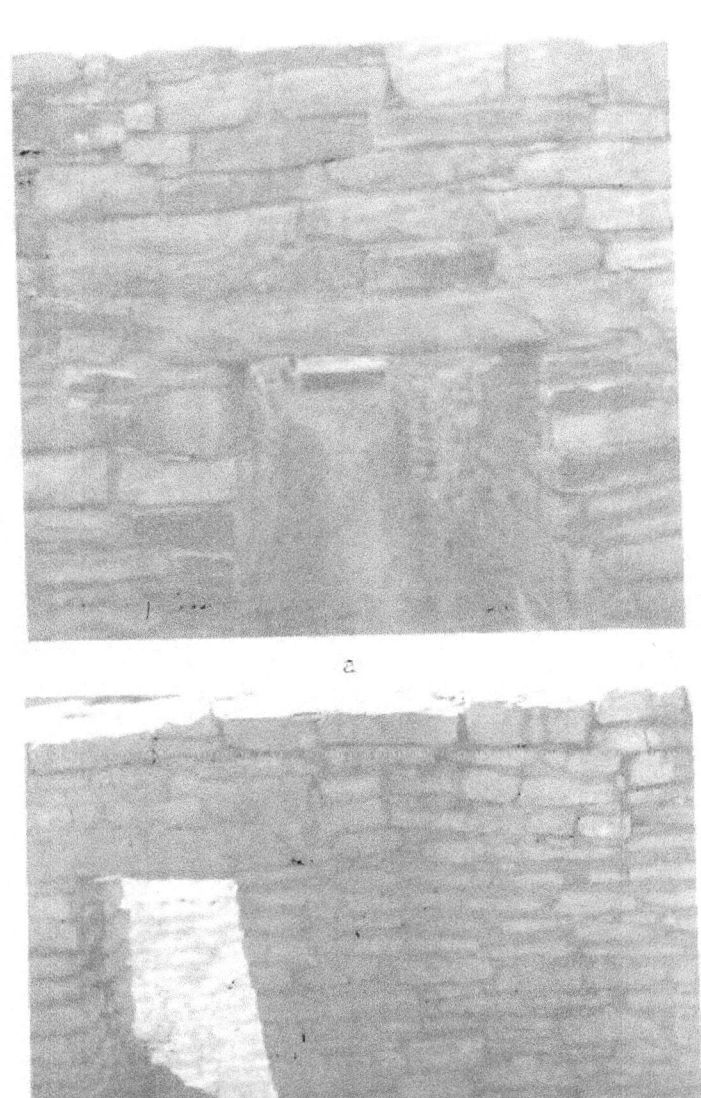

a

b

Figure 5. Doorways stabilized by Ben Williford, 1936. a, Room 10, east doorway; b, Room 10, west doorway.

a

b

Figure 6. Room 9, north exterior wall, 1966. a, before stabilization; b, after stabilization.

a

b

Figure 7. Lowry Pueblo, south end, 1966-67. a, before stabilization;
b, after stabilization; Kiva H is not stabilized in this photo.

a

b

Figure 8. Great Kiva, 1967. a, southeast view before stabilization; b, east view during stabilization.

three doorways and one window. Walls that were in good condition were capped with a two-course cap; in many areas the walls had to be rebuilt partially or completely. Caps were sloped to drain water away from wall junctures. Walls were reconstructed with flat caps and the walls stepped up or down at wall junctures, primarily for safety, since visitiors were unattended at Lowry. Plugged doorways were partially or completely cleared and reconstructed. Walls with large joints resulting from crumbling prehistoric mortar were grouted with cement. Rooms 22, 23, 24 and 25 were excavated to the floors; (Martin had only traced the tops of walls to get dimensions). Rooms either were shallowed out in the center for drainage or drained out a doorway. After the walls were reconstructed, they were coated with a soil paint.

The Great Kiva walls were rebuilt to the ground surface with all moisture drained away from the top of the Kiva. All built-in features were repaired, with drainage to the main part of the Kiva. The poles were replaced in the steps. Rooms 1, 2, and 3 north of the Kiva were reconstructed with low walls of several courses (Fig. 9).

On October 17, 1967, after restoration and stabilization by Al Lancaster and his crew, Lowry Pueblo was dedicated as a National Historic Landmark (Figs. 10-11).

After 1967, an information box was set up over the areas of Kivas A and B explaining that kivas below the surface had painted walls and describing them with photographs. Visitors at Lowry repeatedly expressed an interest in seeing the murals. This, in additon to the need for maintenance stabilization, instigated further work at Lowry.

In 1974, the current project was begun. The maintenance stabilization primarily involved repairing areas of walls where prehistoric mortar was crumbling from runoff beneath cement caps. Several walls were undermined and others had lateral separation. Reconstruction of these areas is discussed in the second half of this report.

Excavation of Kivas A and B began on the east and west sides of the area above the Kivas. Workers cut inward to locate the walls of Kiva A. The inside of Kiva A was then cleared to a depth of 60-85 cm. A test area was dug in the east half of Kiva B to locate the murals. This area was excavated to the floor level; only patches of white plaster with no design remained in this area (Fig. 12). The murals on the north side of Kiva B remained since this area was never excavated by Martin; he ran a tunnel to the north wall to determine the northern boundary of Kiva B, but left a balk between the third and sixth pilasters.

The location of the kivas within the room block, the depth of 4-5m. (17 feet), and the instability of remnant Kiva A walls above Kiva B walls presented immediate problems with removal of the fill. All Kiva A walls that were unstable and a risk to those working in Kiva B were removed. A slide was built from the west wall of Room 3 to the west wall of Room 5

15

a

b

Figure 9. Great Kiva, 1967. a, room block to north during
stabilization; b, walls were stabilized higher to the inside
to drain water outward away from walls.

16

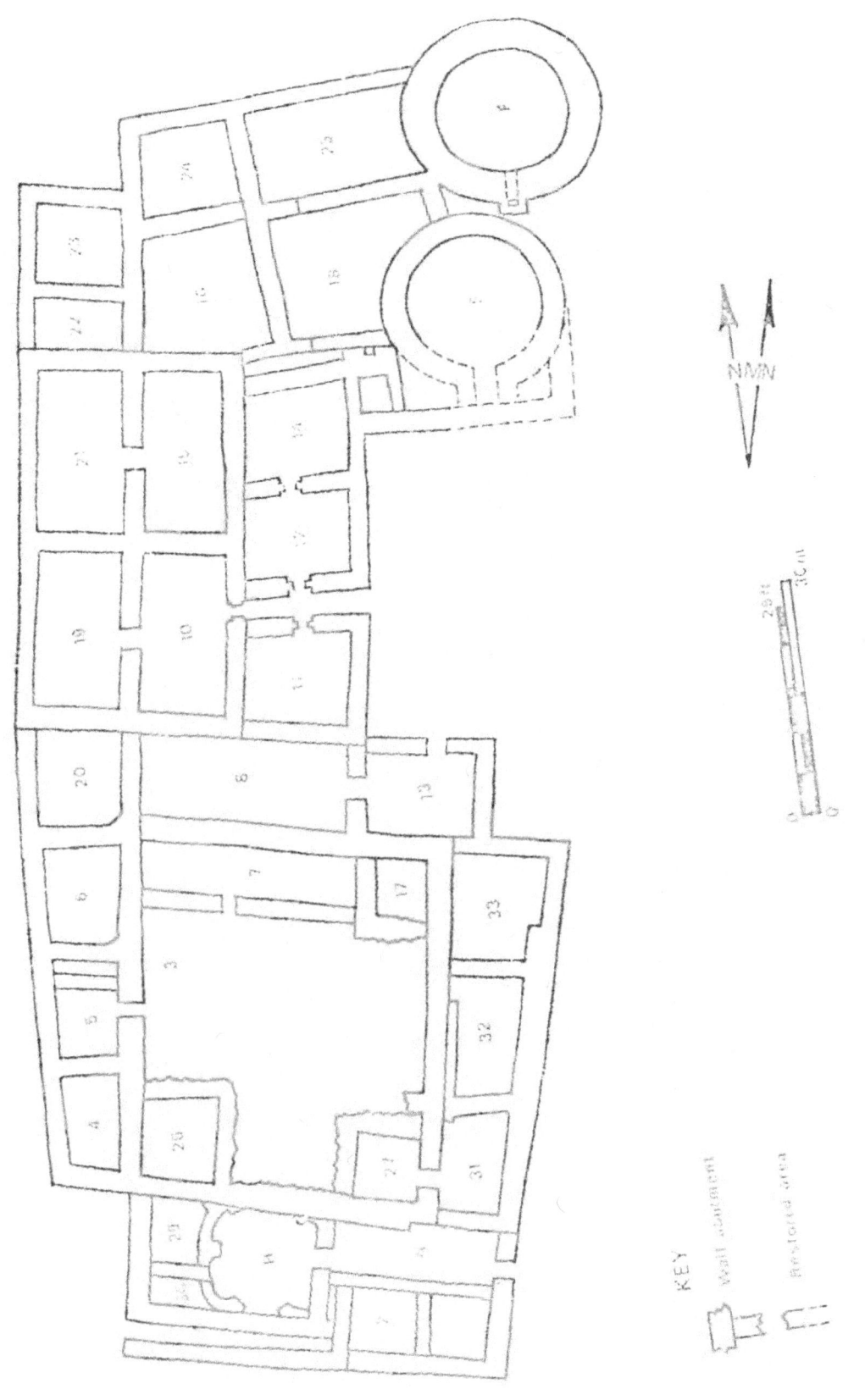

Figure 10. Lowry Pueblo, plan of Lancaster's stabilization, 1966-67.

KEY

Wall treatment

Restored area

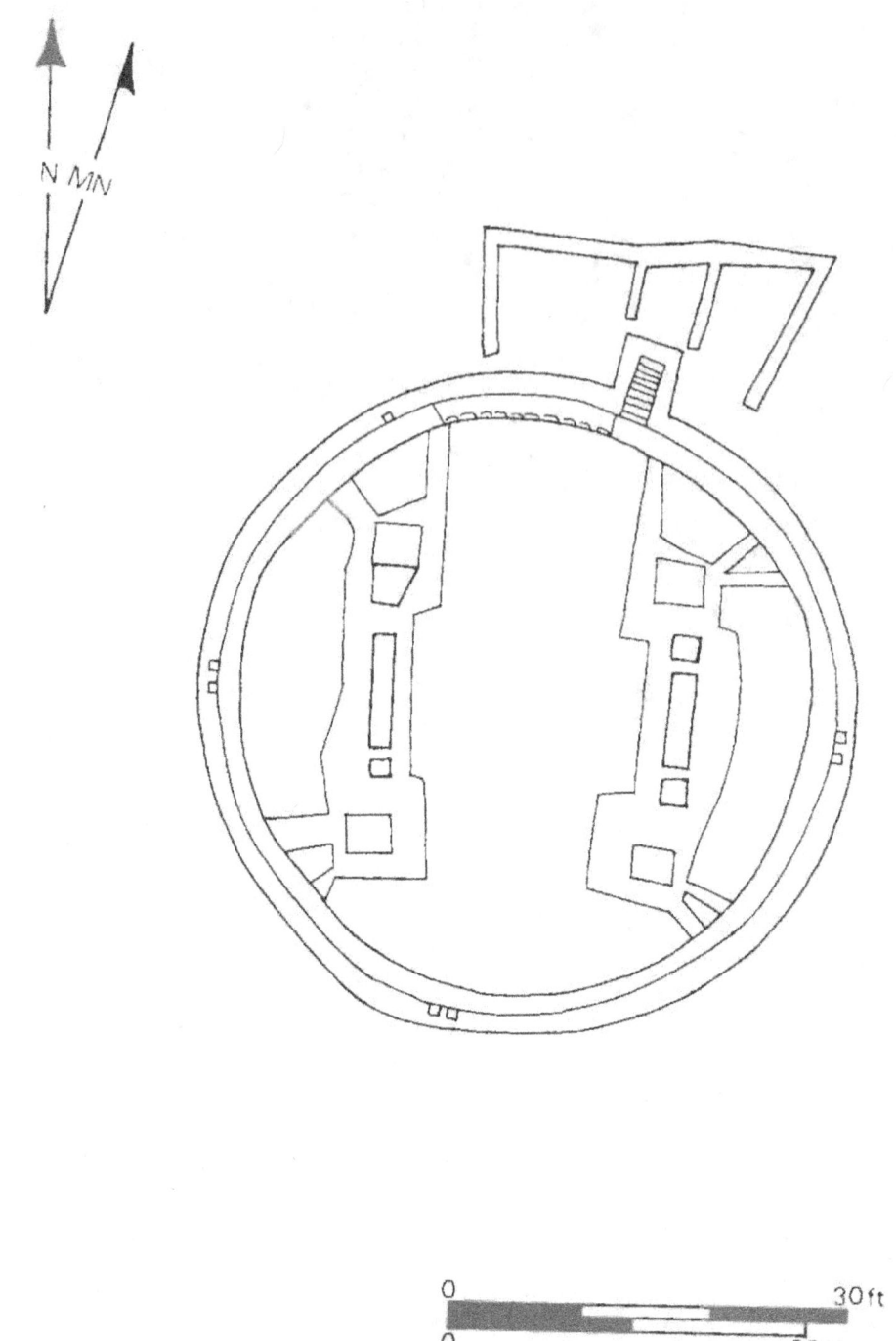

Figure 11. Great Kiva, plan of Lancaster's stabilization.

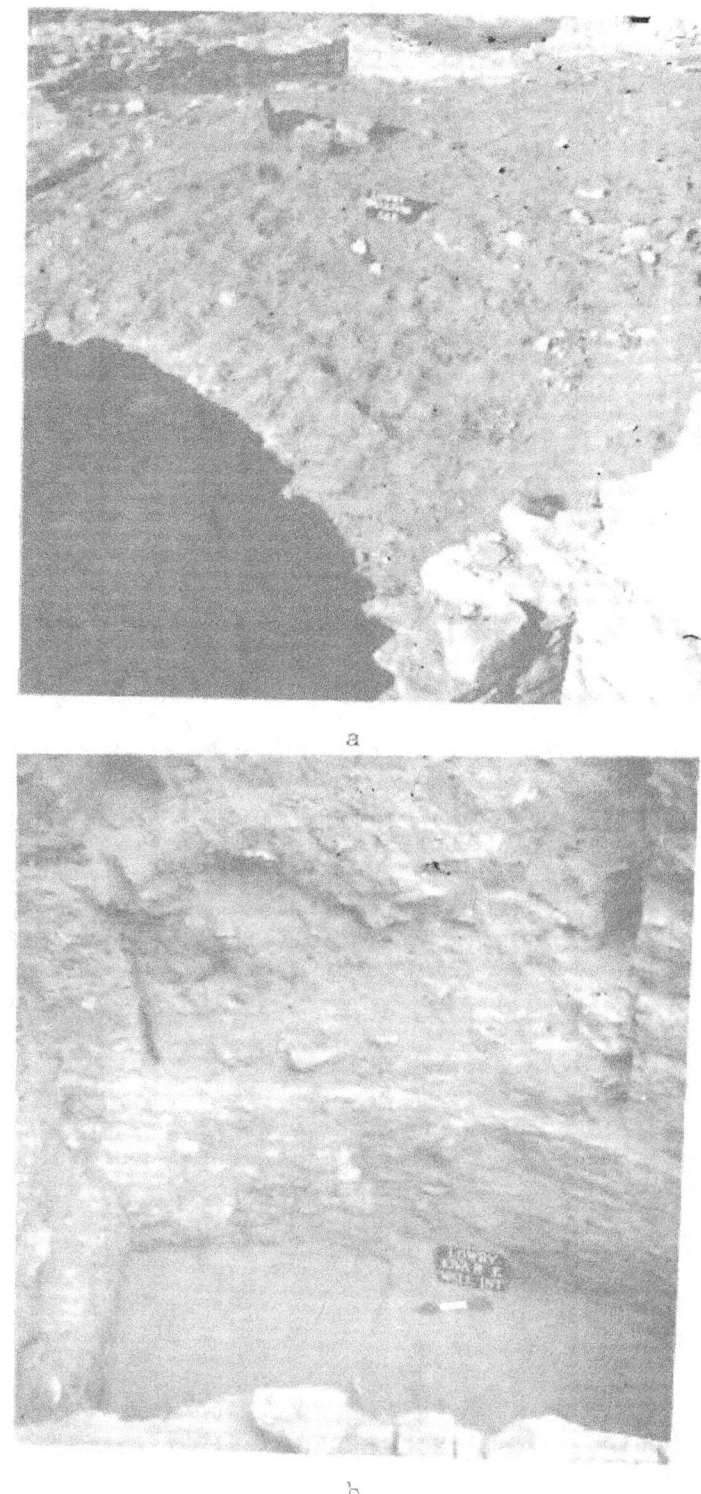

a

b

Figure 12. Kivas A and B. a, filled area above kivas before excavation; b, east side of Kiva B excavated to the floor (plaster has slumped off in this area).

19

to allow dirt to pile on the west side of Room 5. The use of a slide would have saved man-hours, but it did not work and was replaced by a wheelbarrow ramp due to the wetness of the fill. The ramp was supported by a scaffold in Room 5; it allowed the dirt to be thrown into wheelbarrows that were then wheeled to the end of the ramp (Fig. 13). As the depth of Kiva B increased workers had to shovel up to Room 3; from there the fill was shoveled to wheelbarrows, then dumped.

The wheelbarrow ramp extended from the west wall of Room 3 to 60cm west of Room 5. All the boards except the stop were left uncut, since the ramp was serving a temporary function, and would later be dismantled and the lumber used again. The following materials were used:

Platform	4 - 2" x 12"
Stop	1 - 2" x 6"
Legs	4 - 2" x 8"
	2 - 2" x 8"
Bracing	6 - 1" x 6"

With the excavation of Kiva B the walls of Kiva A were almost completely removed, with only a small area remaining on the west side. Kiva B was excavated to 5-10cm above the floor. The benches were cleaned and the murals were photographed (Fig. 14). The condition of the murals was excellent in the areas that had not previously been excavated. Those areas that were lacquered showed damage primarily between the first and second pilasters. Painting the murals with shellac created a hard frontal surface which caused the plaster to separate from the stone wall and other layers of plaster. The presence of moisture, dirt, and roots behind these separated areas increased deterioration. When these areas were excavated, the plaster either crumbled or gradually began to break down as it dried out; no successful process has been discovered to stop this type of deterioration.

In order to recover as much of the design as possible, tracings were taken of the murals in sections. The tracings show what design remains, the areas cracked, and in some instances a previous design where the plaster had broken off. Close-up photographs were also taken of the entire bench (Fig. 15). A color sample was taken of the plaster. As soon as the murals were recorded, they were covered with strips of plastic sheeting, which were anchored to the tops of surrounding walls and draped down over the murals (Fig. 16).

Kiva B, Temporary Roof

The final work at Lowry in 1974 was a temporary roof providing protection against the winter. There were several problems associated with the construction of a temporary roof over Kiva B. The west wall of Kiva B was not exposed; fill and a remnant wall of Kiva B remained. The upper course of the east wall was exposed. The difference in height was approximately 1m. from west to east; this created a room with a pitch

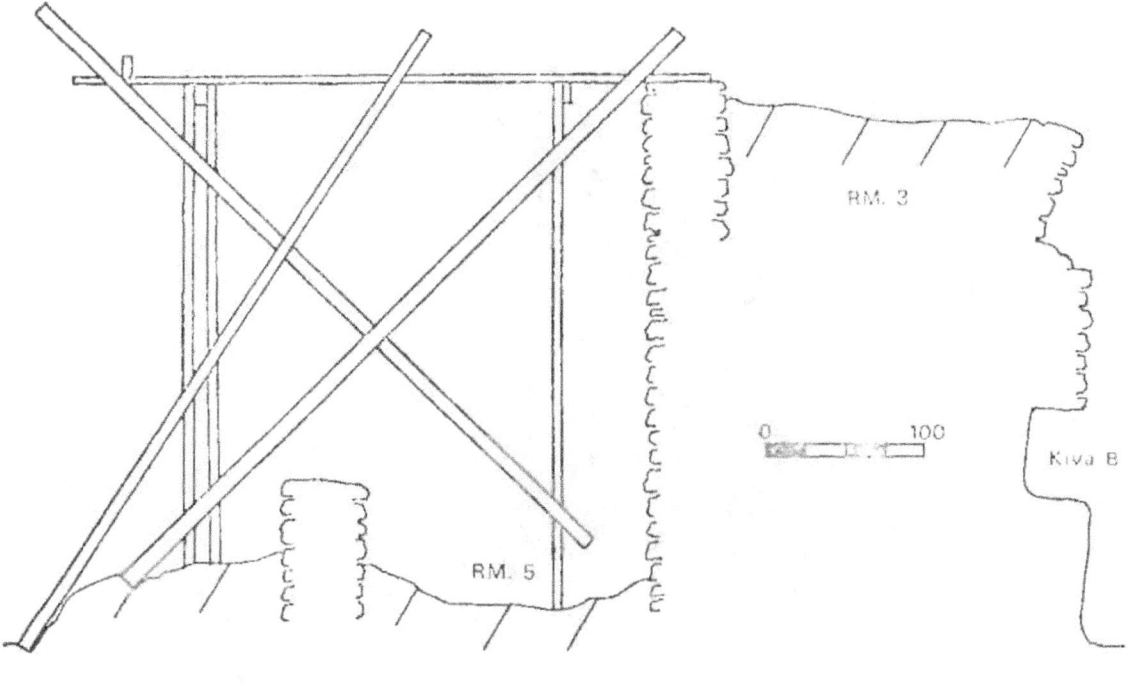

a

b

Figure 13. Kiva B, wheelbarrow ramp. a, east-west profile of ramp in relationship to Kiva B; b, photograph looking southwest, Kiva B in foreground.

21

a

b

Figure 14. Kiva B. a, north view of murals after excavation in 1974; b, close-up of damaged area where plaster is peeling from the walls.

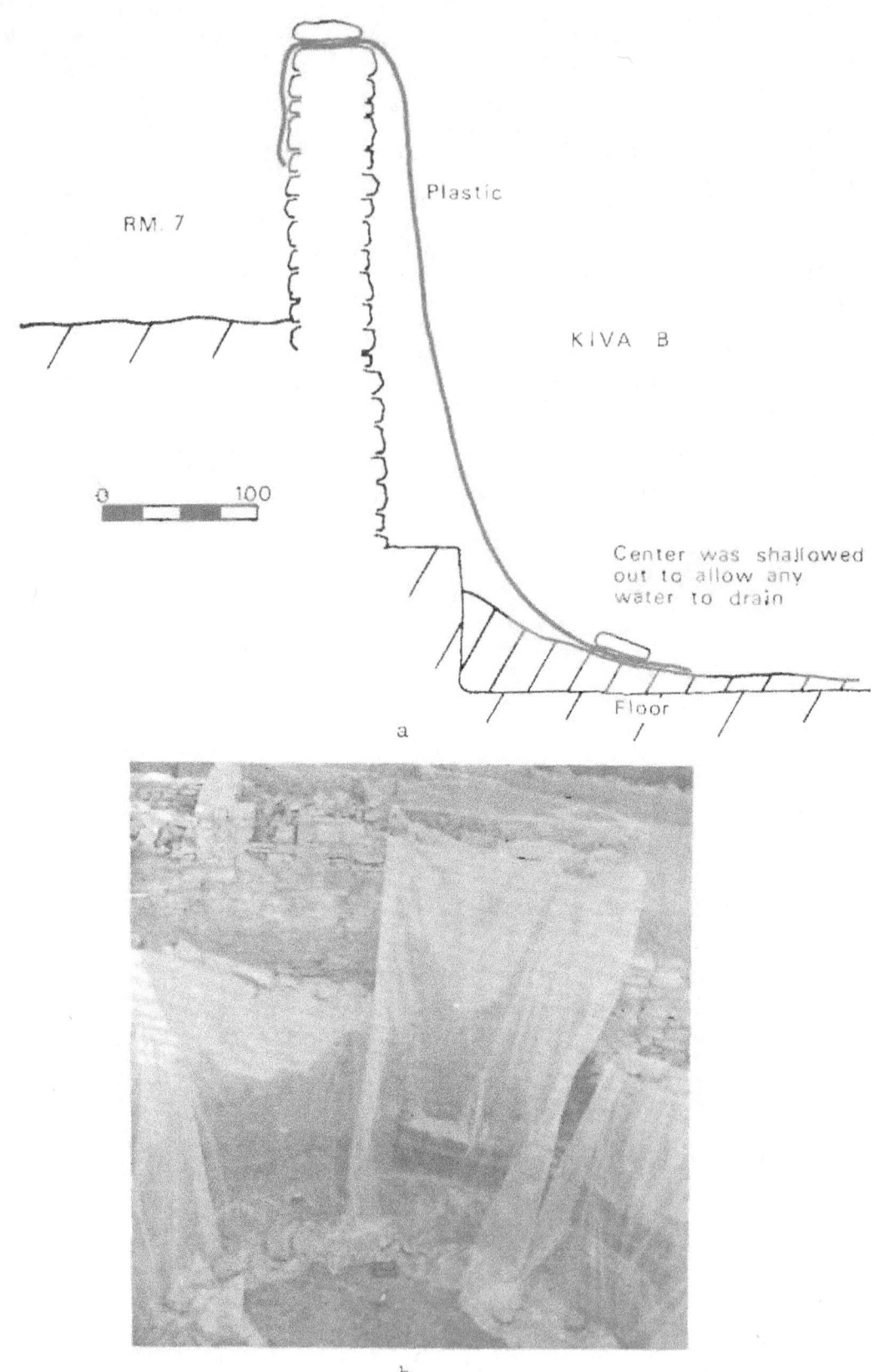

RM. 7

Plastic

KIVA B

0   100

Center was shallowed
out to allow any
water to drain

Floor

a

b

Figure 16. Kiva B. a, north-south profile of plastic sheeting
over murals; b, north view of plastic sheeting secured with stones
to the top of surrounding walls and draped over murals.

of 4:1 (Fig. 17). Since the roof would be built on fill and unstabilized walls, bracing inside the Kiva was necessary. Roof drainage was into the unnumbered space east of Kiva B; any moisture that collected in the space could seep down the walls and cause undermining. The shape of the roof had to allow for the southern recess, and the 1.5 - 1.8m. difference between the north wall and the south wall of Room 7 (Fig. 18).

The following description of the temporary roof construction is divided into structural sections, by construction sequence.

Roof Frame:

Plates: Two plates of four 2" x 12" spliced boards were secured parallel to the outside of the east and west walls of Kiva B. The plates were nailed at the north and south to juniper posts that were secured in the fill. The plate on the west side was placed approximately 60cm above the fill. A dry wall was built between the fill and plate to add support. The east plate was placed on the same level as the top course of the east wall of Kiva B.

Rafters: Nine rafters 25' in length were constructed of 2" x 12" or 2" x 8". Two boards of either size were spliced with a scab nailed to the side. The rafters spanned the kiva east-west on two-foot centers, alternating between 2" x 12" or 8" rafters. Each end butted up against and was nailed to the plates. On the east side the rafters rested on the wall of Kiva B. The area over the southern recess was boxed in with two shorter rafters.

Dry Wall: Dry wall was used to seal open areas between the plates and fill or walls, which added support and sealed the kiva against moisture and vandals. Plastic was placed against the dry wall on the west and south sides, then banked with dirt as an additional protection against moisture, since the dry wall was built on fill in these two areas.

Nailers: Boards of 1" x 4" were used as nailers for the corrugated tin roof. The boards were laid horizontally across the rafters and plates on 2' centers (Fig. 19).

Vertical Support Braces:

Vertical support was given to all rafters at the splice and at half the distance from the splice to the west plate (Fig. 17). Two 2" x 8" strips were nailed across the bottom of the rafters at the splice and the other areas of braces. Braces were of 2" x 8" and 2" x 6" boards with various sized scraps as a base on the ground surface of Kiva B. The braces were sprung into place.

Roof:

The roof was constructed of 2' x 12' sections of corrugated tin. The tin was nailed to the nailers with the first sections beginning on the east

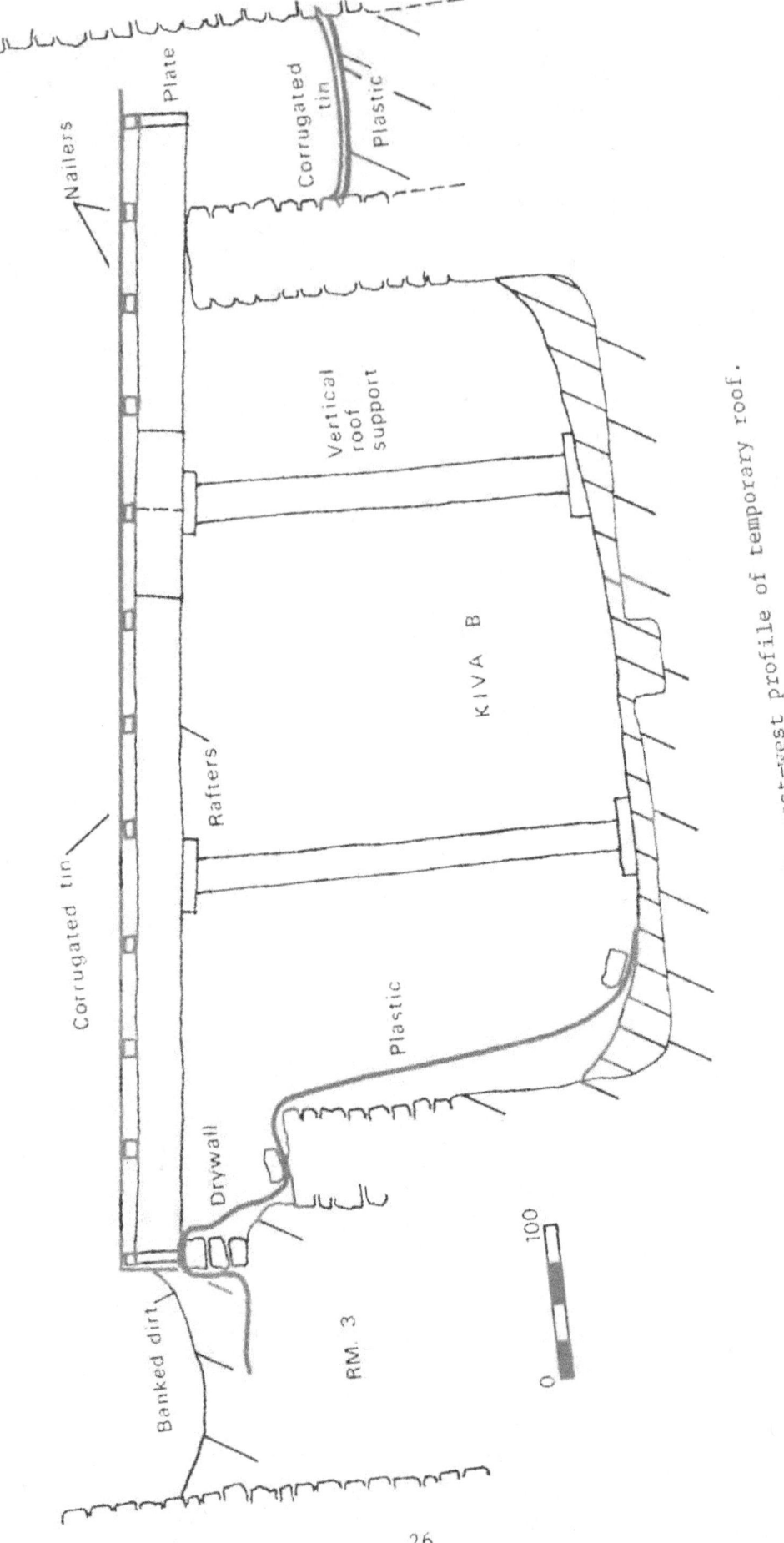

Figure 17. Kiva B, east-west profile of temporary roof.

Nailers

Plate

Corrugated tin

Plastic

Corrugated tin

Vertical roof support

Rafters

KIVA B

Plastic

Drywall

Banked dirt

RM. 3

100

0

26

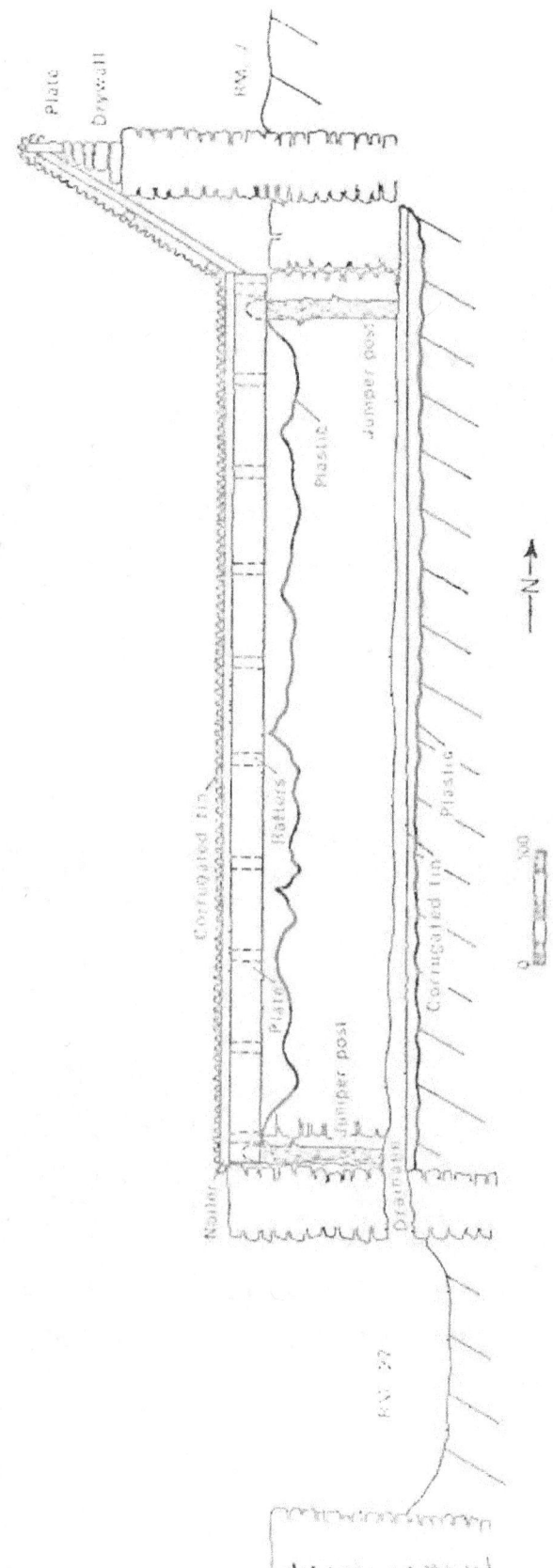

Figure 18. Kiva B, north-south profile of temporary roof.

27

a

b

Figure 19. Kiva B. a, north view of roof frame, temporary roof;
b, north view of corrugated tin roof.

side (drainage of roof was to the east). The sections were overlapped
from the north to the south 3". Then the second and third rows were
overlapped to the east (Fig. 19). Most of the drainage from the roof went
into the space east of Kiva B. Plastic was put on the ground with
corrugated tin over it. The tin was sloped to the south so the water went
through a hole in the north wall of Room 27 into the center of the room
(Fig. 18).

Wing Roof:

A wing roof was built from the north wall of Kiva B to the south wall of
Room 7 to close the distance of 1.5m to 2m in height between the two walls.
A 2" x 12" plate was secured with juniper posts horizontally along with
the south wall of Room 7. Rafters of 2" x 4" boards were cut at different
lengths and at different angles to toe in with the roof; they were placed
on 2' centers. Nailers on 2' centers extended east-west across the
rafters. The roof of corrugated tin sections overlapped from the east
to the west 3" with drainage downward onto Kiva B. Plastic cement was
used to seal the area where the wing roof met the main roof, and around
nail holes (Fig. 19). The wing roof and Kiva B were completely enclosed
on all sides.

Material List:

    Lumber:

1" x 4" -	392' =	Nailers for Tin
1" x 6" -	48' =	Cross Bracing on Vertical Support Braces
2" x 4" -	140' =	Wing Roof Rafters
2" x 6" -	60' =	Vertical Support Braces; Brace Blocks
2" x 8" -	350' =	Rafters; Vertical Support Braces
2" x 12"-	208' =	Rafters

        Total Board Ft. <u>1,198</u>

    <u>Nails</u>:

Roof Tacks 9 ½ lbs.		= Tin Nailers
8d	4 lbs.	= Nailers to Rafters
10d	5 lbs.	= Rafter Splices
16d	8 lbs.	= Frame
16d cc	10 lbs.	= Frame

    <u>Corrugated Tin</u>:   30 - 2' x 12' Steel Plates

    <u>Plastic Cement</u>:   1 gallon

    <u>Plastic Sheeting</u>:   1 roll of 200 sq. ft.
                                1 roll of 1,000 sq. ft.

Kiva B and Room 27, 1975

In the spring of 1975, the first work at Lowry was the removal of the temporary roof so that restoration (Reports 23-25, 27-33, 35) of Kiva B could begin. After restoration, access to Kiva B and a permanent roof would be built.

Creating an access entryway into Kiva B involved excavation, construction of two doorways, steps, and two retaining walls.

The access began at Room 31. Beam steps of 90cm in length by 1.2m in width, on a stone foundation, lead down into Room 31 (Fig. 20). This room and Room 27 were both excavated to a depth of 90-1.2m to provide higher doorways, to lessen accidents. The restoration of the entryway to Room 27 is covered in Report 34. The drainage hole in the north wall of Room 27 was enlarged to create a doorway built with wooden lintels (Fig. 20). This doorway led into the south end of the unnumbered space east of Kiva B. The south end was excavated to a depth of 70 cm with a retaining wall built to hold back the fill of the rest of the area. This wall is 75cm high and spans the distance between the east wall of Kiva B and the west all of Room 32. A small wing wall was constructed to span the distance between the northwest exterior corner of Room 27 and the exterior southeast wall of Kiva B (Fig. 21).

An entrance to Kiva B was built through the east side of the southern recess. Building stones were removed from the wall to create a rough doorway; care was taken to keep the sides straight (Fig. 22). Two steps of flagstone were built in the doorway. The steps were laid in a bed of cement with a veneer under each step (Fig. 23). Both sides of the entryway were finished by veneering the sough side to a depth of 64cm and 1.8m in height, and the north side to a depth of 25cm and a height of 1.75m (Fig. 22).

A gate constructed of ½" rebar was placed across the southern recess to allow visitors to view the Kiva but not enter (Fig. 24). A three-four course single wall of 67cm was built to span the vent shaft to show its presence. Reconstruction was impossible since visitors stand directly over the shaft in the southern recess.

Precautions against the problems encountered with the temporary roof were taken into account with the construction of the permanent roof. The problem of loose fill on the west and south sides was remedied with the construction of retaining walls. The remnant of the west wall of Kiva A was reconstructed (Report 35) to extend along the west wall of Room 3 from north to south. The retaining wall was built across the area above the southern recess of Kiva B; a wall was also built on a remnant wall of Kiva A. 60-75cm were added to the top of the east wall of Kiva B; this addition decreased the pitch of the permanent roof to 2" - 12" (Figs. 25-26).

a

b

Figure 20. Rooms 31 and 27. a, Room 31, view of beam steps; b, Room 27, entrance in north wall.

a

b

Figure 21. Wing Wall connecting northwest exterior corner of Room
27 and Kiva 8. a, fill area before wall was constructed; b, after
construction of wall.

Figure 22. Kiva B, veneered doorway through southern recess.

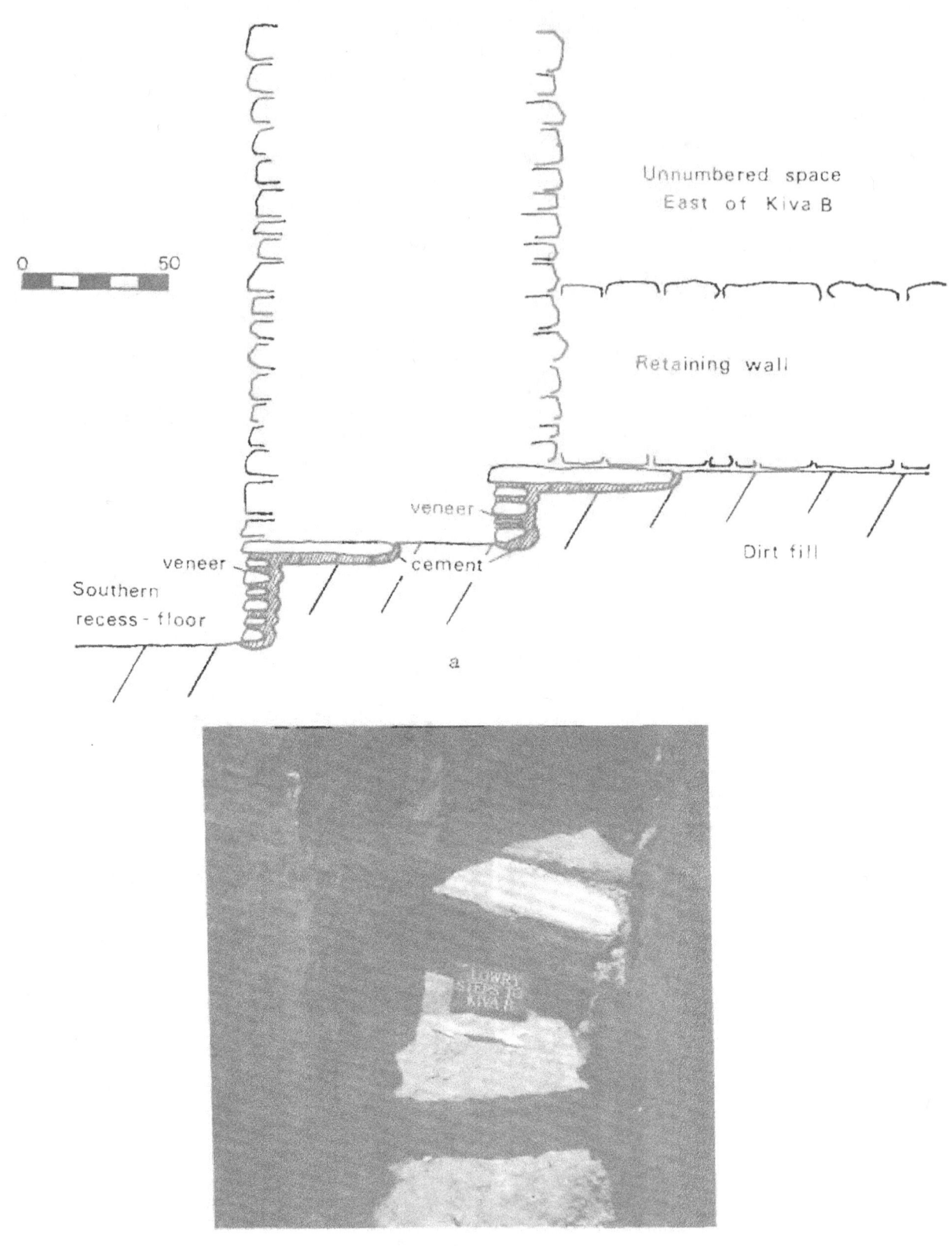

Unnumbered space
East of Kiva B

Retaining wall

veneer

Dirt fill

veneer

cement

Southern
recess - floor

a

b

Figure 23. Kiva B, entryway through southern recess. a, east—west
profile of flagstone steps; b, east view after construction.

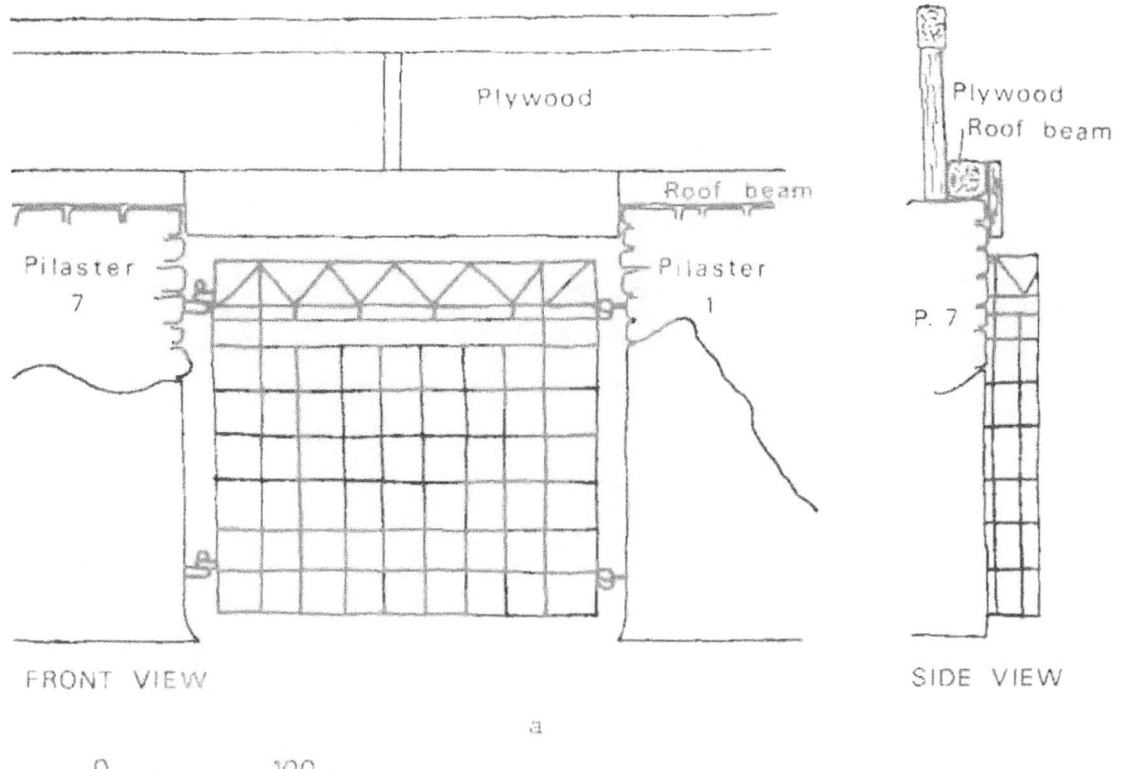

Plywood

Roof beam

Pilaster 7

Pilaster 1

P. 7

FRONT VIEW

SIDE VIEW

a

0   100

b

Figure 24. Kiva B, rebar gate. a, front and side profiles; b, south view of gate.

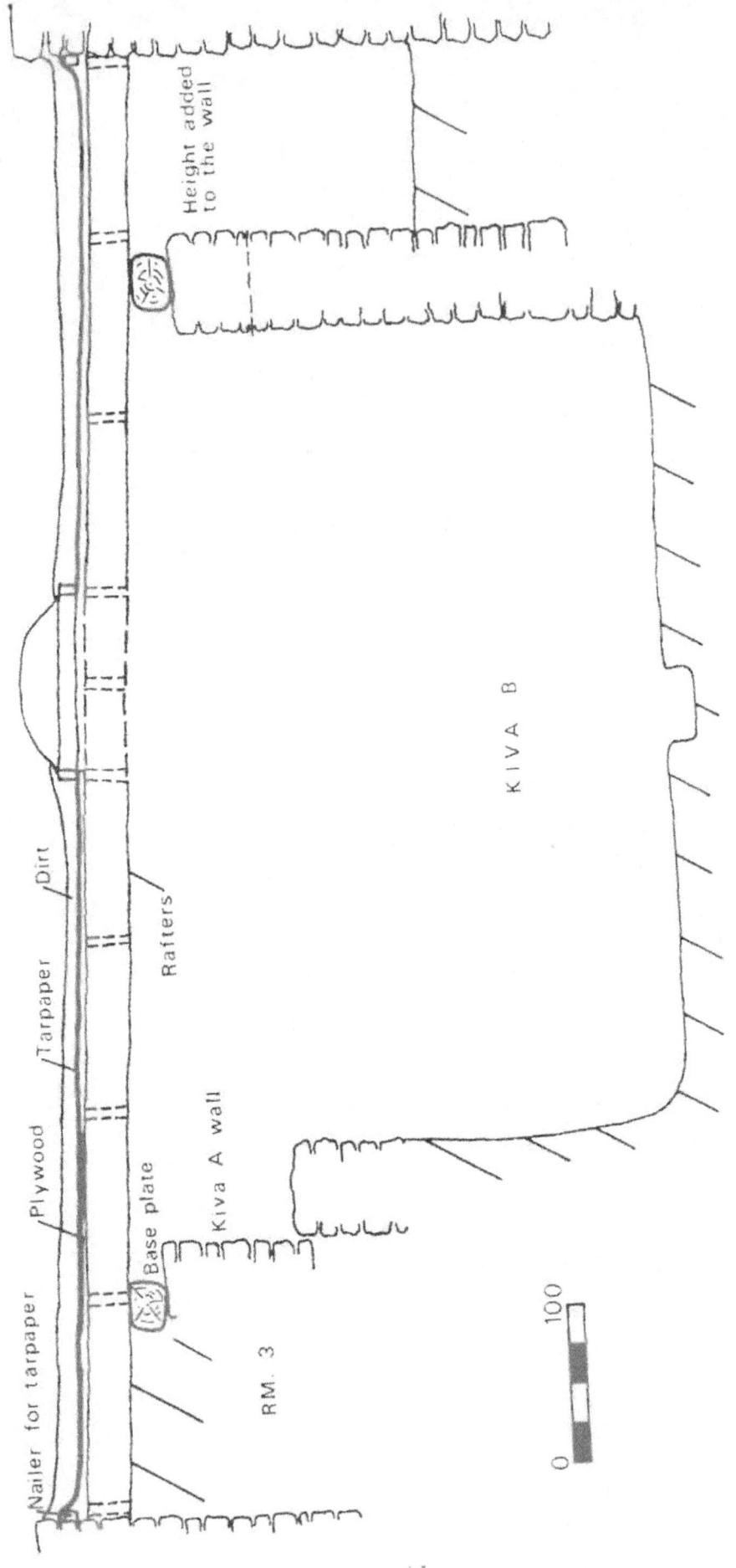

Figure 25. Kiva B, east-west profile of permanent roof.

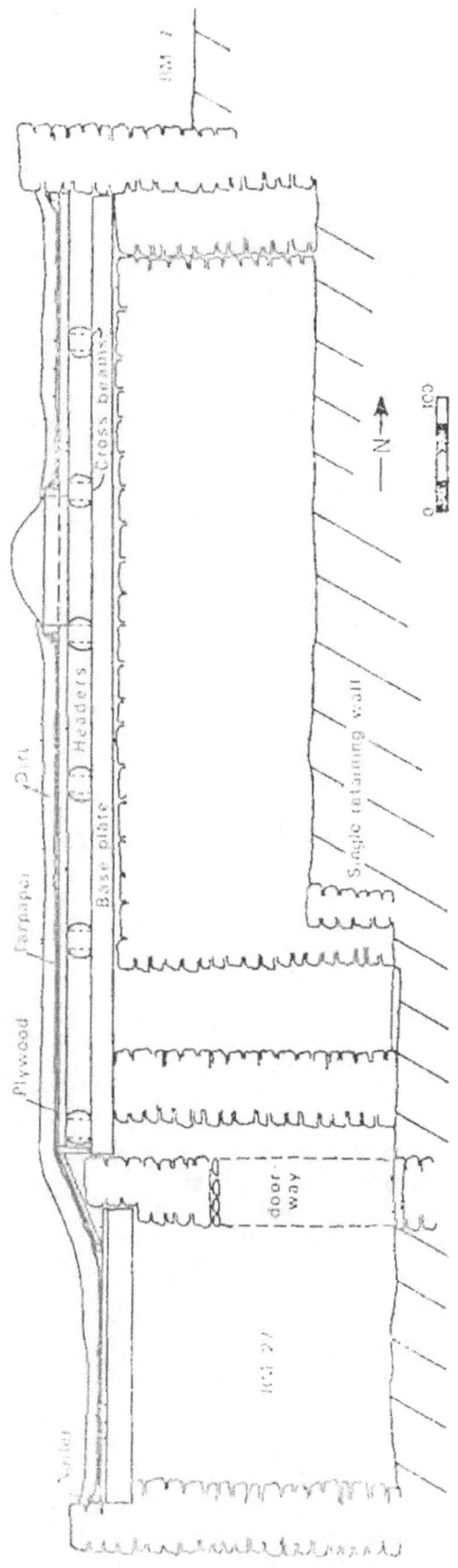

Figure 26. Kiva B, north-south profile of permanent roof.

37

The permanent roof construction is divided into structural sections, by construction sequence.

Roof Frame:

Base plates: Two 4" x 8" x 34' beams were used for the base plates. The plates rested on the west wall of Kiva A and the east wall of Kiva B. The plates were tilted to conform to the pitch of the roof and then secured in several areas with cement.

Rafters: Five 8" x 8" x 34' beams were placed on four-foot centers across Kiva B. The beams rested on the base plates and butted up to the west wall of Room 3 and the east wall of the space east of Kiva B. Two shorter beams were used at the north and south ends across the southern recess and against the south wall of Room 7. The rafters were nailed to the base plates with 1' bridge spikes (Fig. 27).

Frame Nailers: Nailers of 2" x 8" boards were placed in chiseled sockets on four-foot centers between all the rafters (Fig. 27).

Roof:

Plywood: Sheets of 4' x 8' plywood were nailed to the roof frame length-wise north-south. The rows were staggered to give the seams more strength (Fig. 27).

Plastic Bubble: A four-foot frame of 2" x 4" was built as a base for the skylight. The frame was secured on top of the plywood. The bubble was then screwed to the frame (Fig. 28).

Tarpaper Nailers: 1" x 4" boards were nailed around the edge of the roof as nailers for the tarpaper and as additional sealers against moisture (Fig. 27).

Tarpaper: Strips of tarpaper were laid over the plywood and secured to the nailers. Plastic roofing was used to seal the joints around the edges of the roof and particularly around the bubble (Fig. 29).

Dirt: 10-15cm of dirt were put on the roof (Fig. 29). A drainage pipe was screwed with a coupling into the southeast corner of the roof that extended 90-15cm below the surface, made a 90° turn, and extended along the north wall of Room 31 to 8m beyond the Pueblo. A drainage box was placed over the pipe into the roof (Fig. 30). The pipe was wrapped in insulation and the portion left exposed was covered with a plywood box.

Material list:

Lumber:	1" x 4" -	464'	= Nailers for Tarpaper
	2" x 4" -	160'	= Miscellaneous Bracing
	2" x 6" -	400'	= Wing Wall
	2" x 8" -	1736'	= Frame Nailers
	Total Board Feet	2660	

a

b

Figure 27. Kiva B, permanent roof. a, north view of roof frame;
b, north view of plywood roof and frame nailers.

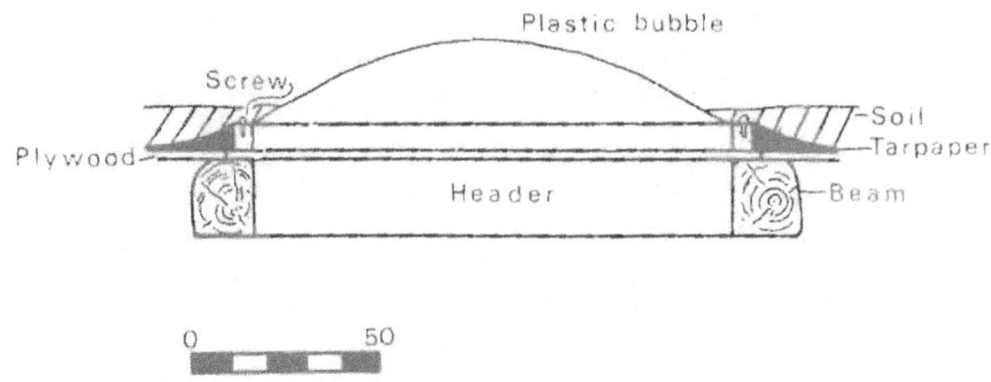

Plastic bubble

Screw

Plywood

Soil

Tarpaper

Header

Beam

0   50

a

b

Figure 28.   Kiva B, permanent roof.   a, profile of plastic bubble;
b, northeast view of plastic bubble secured to roof.

40

| Dry Spruce Timber: | 8 - 8" x 8" x 34' = Rafters |
| | 2 - 4" x 8" x 34' = Base Plates |

Nails:	# 5/8 6½ lbs. = Tarpaper to Plywood
	8d galv. 13 lbs. = Plywood to Rafters
	"spikes" 12" = Rafters to Base Plates
	20 wood screws = Bubble to 2" x 4" frame

Miscellaneous: 32 sheets of 4' x 8' 3/4 inch plywood, CD
with exterior glue

10 rolls (1 square each) of #65 tarpaper

2 - 5 gal. cans of Albert DS, Semi-gloss
fire retardant for rafters

7 gal. 1 qt. Plastic Roof Cement

4' x 4' Plastic Bubble with 1½" flange

Drainage: 1 roll 4" x 15" F15 Insulation
8 - 10 ft. sections of Plastic 4-inch sewer pipe
1 - 45° coupling for 4-inch sewer pipe
4 - 4" couplings for 4-inch sewer pipe

Room 27 was roofed with Kiva B. Six sockets were chiseled out of the north and south walls for the rafters to rest on; the rafters were three spruce timbers 8'6", 8'9" and 8'11" in length set in a bed of cement. Two sheets of plywood were laid directly on the beams (Fig. 31); a quarter roll of tarpaper was nailed to the nailers. A wing wall of 2" x 6" rafters connected this roof to the roof over Kiva B, making it continuous. It was covered with 10 to 15cm of dirt (Fig. 26).

a

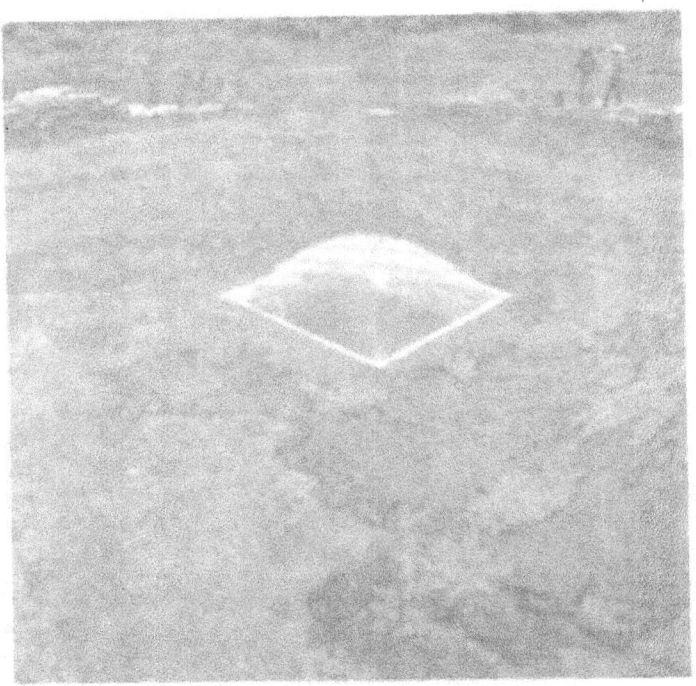

b

Figure 29. Kiva B, permanent roof. a, north view of tarpaper layer and areas sealed with plastic cement; b, after addition of dirt layer.

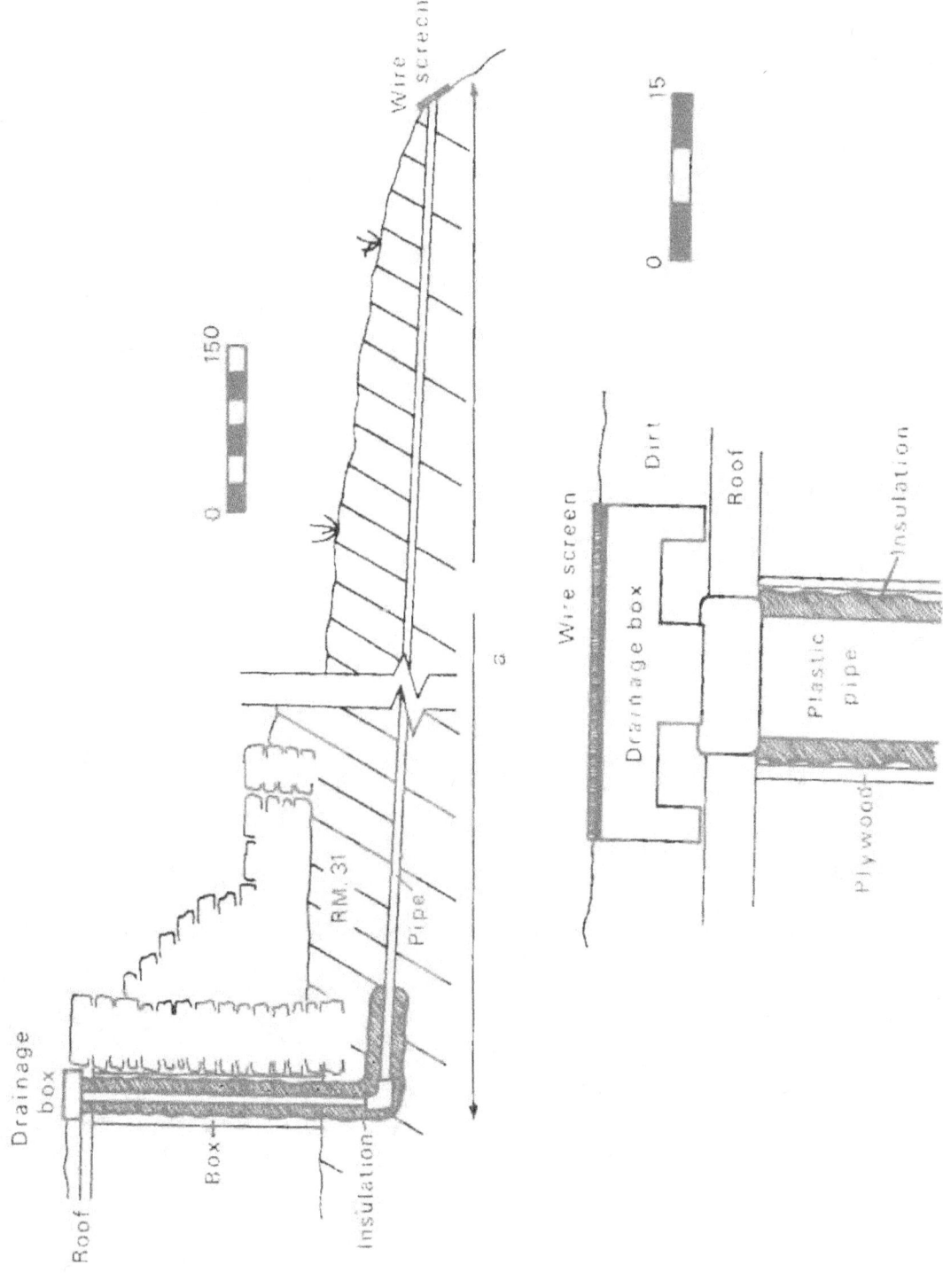

Figure 30. Kiva B, drainage system. a, east-west profile of drainage route; b, east-west profile of drainage box.

43

Each wall that required maintenance stabilization is described in separate reports with before-and-after photographs keyed to Figures 32-33.

Different types of damage are definable into recurring problems that plague surface ruins. There does not appear any feasible way to stabilize a surface ruin other than capping the walls; this leaves most of the original wall intact and above-ground, but requires maintenance stabilization on a regular basis. Most damage occurs at the bond between the cement cap and the prehistoric wall; water runoff down the cement cap onto the prehistoric wall causes gradual erosion of mortar and stone. If moisture enters the core of the wall, lateral separation can occur causing the wall to bulge outward (Report 7); if moisture enters the wall and freezes, cracks and bulging can result. If drainage is shallowing out the center of the room, it must be done again in several years when the area fills in. If the room is allowed to level again, the water can drain toward a wall and cause undermining above and below ground-surface (Report 10).

Visitor traffic through an unattended ruin can be the cause of damage. Walls are climbed on; areas that have been stepped up or down to meet another wall in a fragmented effect are used as steps (Report 3). Rodents burrowing under walls and plant growth can also cause damage (Report 19).

The restoration of Kiva B is also described by report form. Each pilaster is described individually, with other restored features. (Reports 23-25, 27-33, 35).

Walls

The basic materials used in stabilizing the walls of Lowry are the same used by Lancaster in 1966-67. Portland Type I and II cement and Shiprock sand (sharp mortar sand) in a 3:1 proportion with 6 oz. of Tamms mortar coloring light buff added, per 12:4 load, to take some of the blue-green color out of the cement. No new stone was quarried. All cement joints were pointed to a depth of 1.5-3.0cm; joints were filled with soil mortar flush to the stone. Different ratios of soil to sand (4:1, 3:1, 2:1 and 1:0) were tried to make a harder mortar that cracked and shrank less. Different types of manufacture were also attempted: the mortar was kneaded to remove all excess moisture until it had a stiff consistency; in other instances it was applied to the joints while wet and sticky, and allowed to dry out gradually by repeated applications of water. The results were less than desirable for all the ratios and methods. Failure was probably due to a low clay level and high plant content to the soil; it also may be due to rapid dehydration which causes shrinking and cracking

When a wetter mortar was used to plaster and reconstruct a small area of the floor of Kiva B, the result was better. The mortar was spread on and continually smoothed with either the palm of the hand or a trowel. This success may have been due to the shade from the roof, application in a

a

b

Figure 31. Room 27, permanent roof. a, south view of beams set in sockets over room; b, west view of plywood roof.

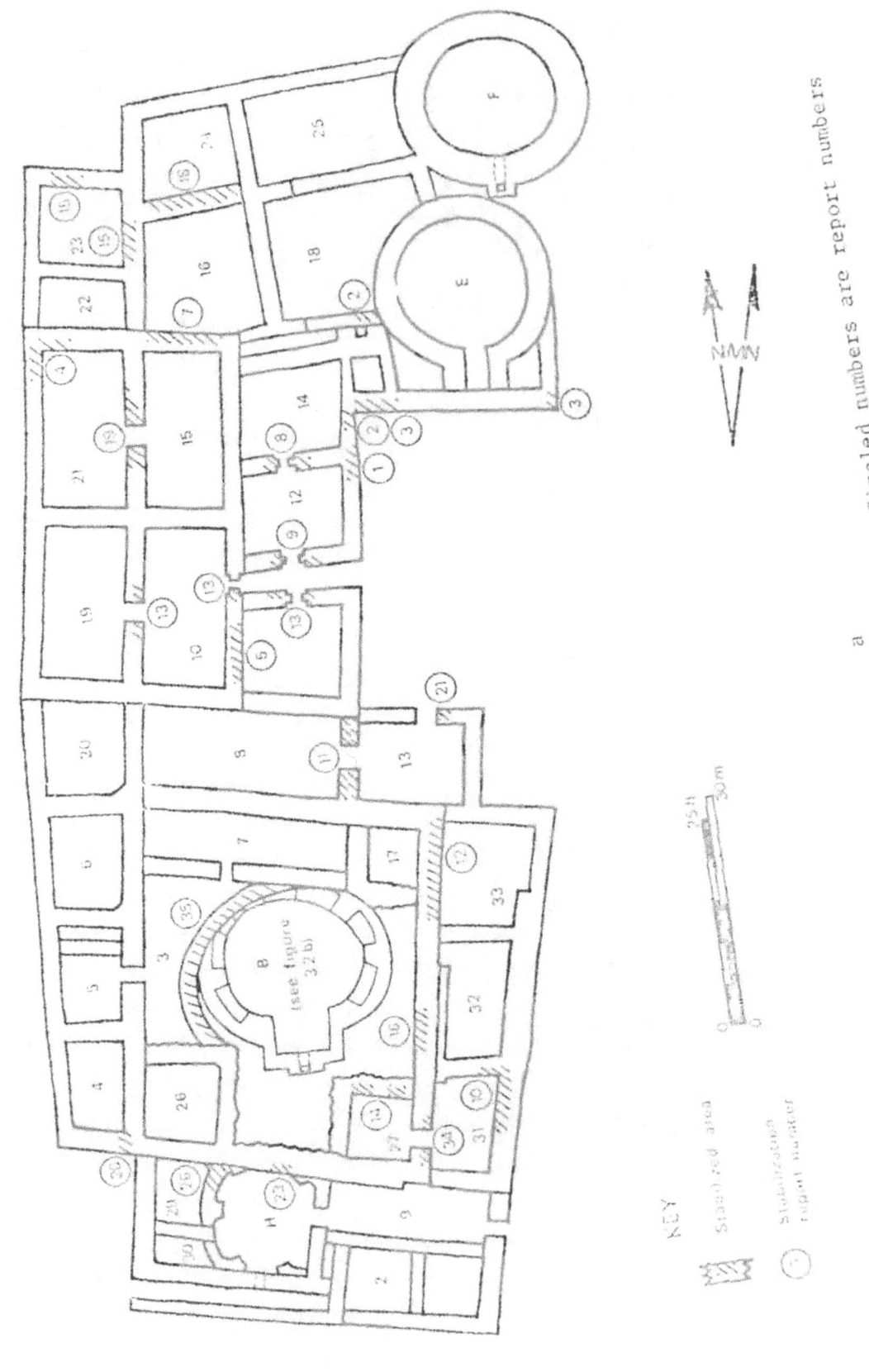

Figure 32a. Lowry Pueblo, plan of CU stabilization.

a   Circled numbers are report numbers

46

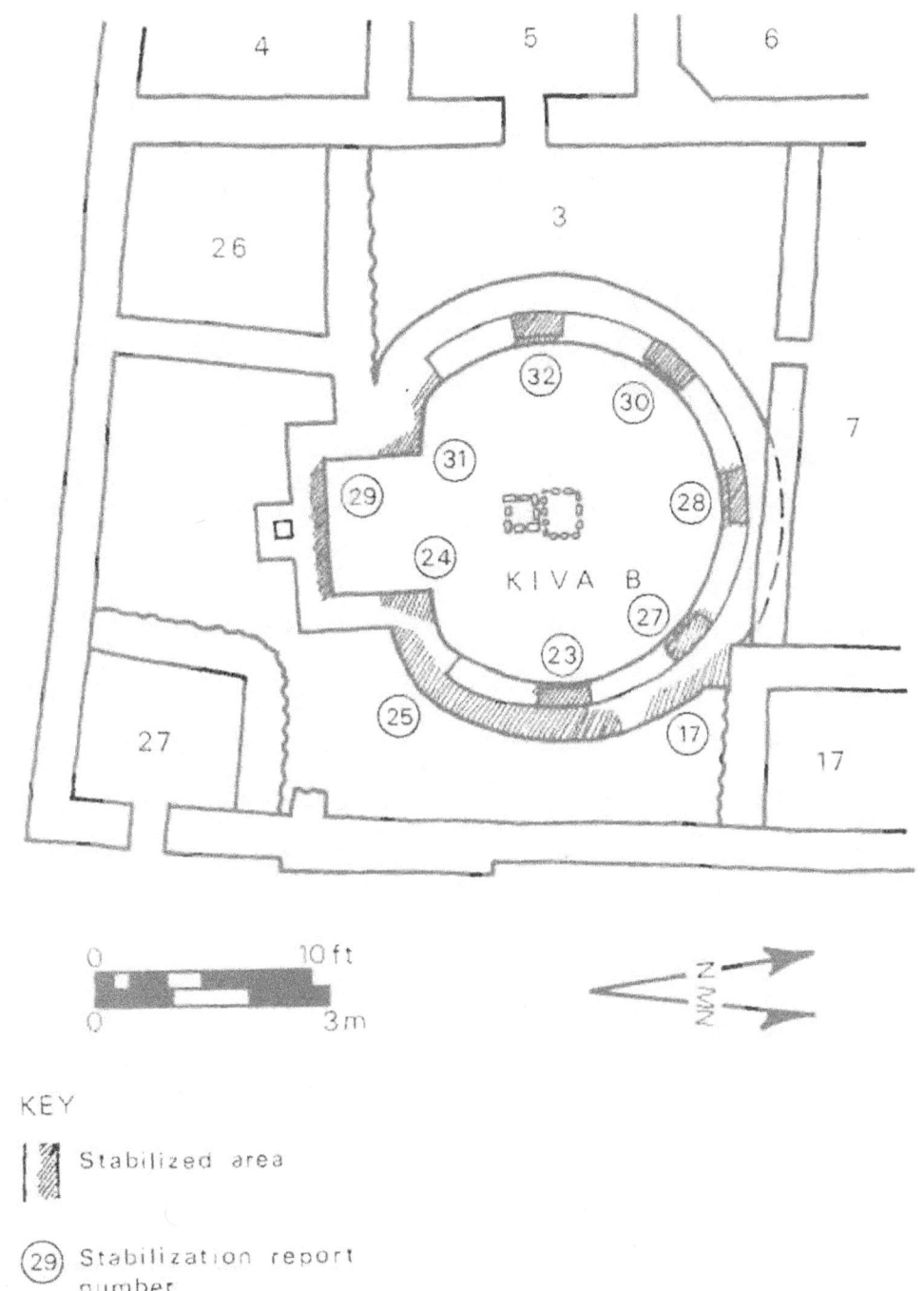

KEY

Stabilized area

(29) Stabilization report
number

Figure 32b. Kiva B, plan of CU stabilization. Circled numbers
are report numbers.

47

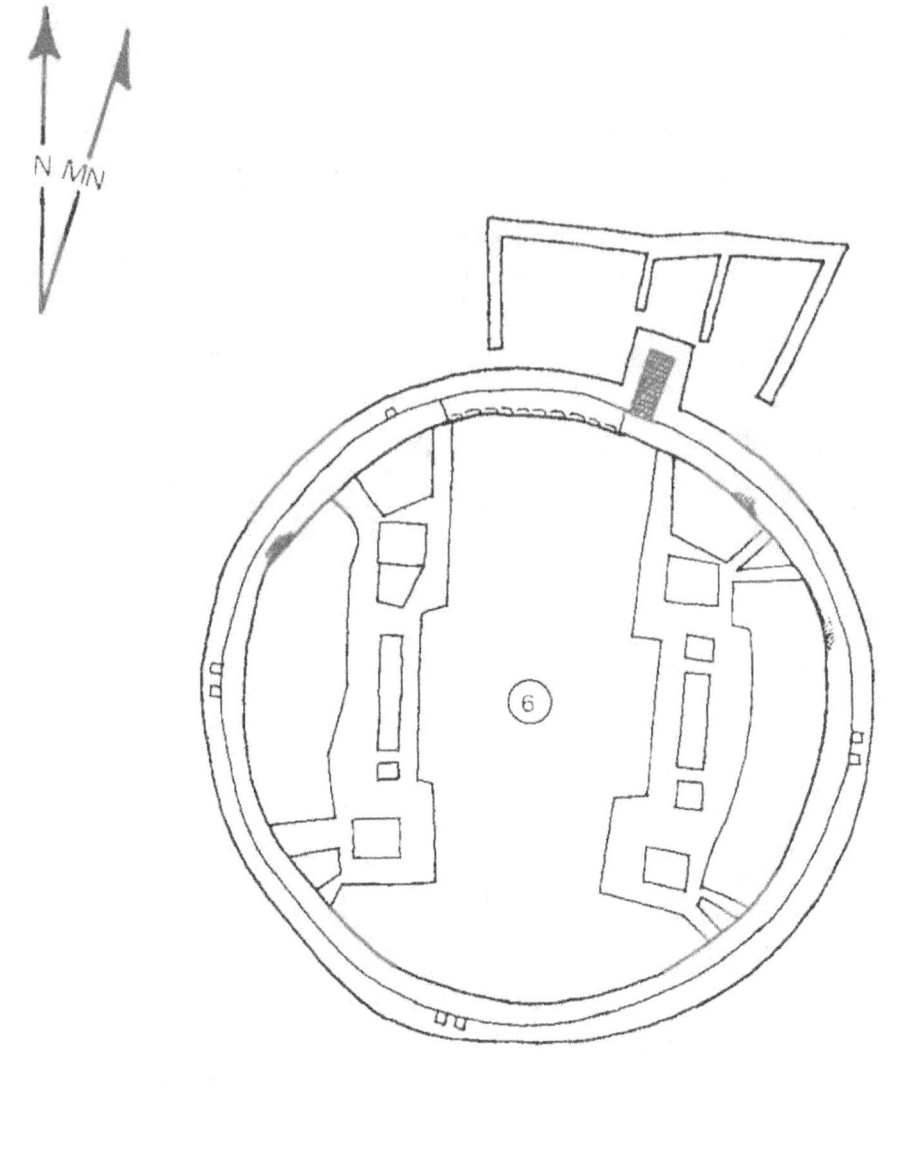

Figure 33. Great Kiva, plan of CU stabilization, circled number
is stabilization report number.

thin layer, continually smoothing of the area, or to all three. A soil cement of two parts oil to one part cement was experimented with slightly (Reports 26 and 36). A small amount of coloring was added to the mixture to counteract some of the cement coloring, but the result was still far too gray. Soil cement has strength, does not crack, and shrinking is minimal. If a white cement was used, with some experimentation, a desirable color probably could be obtained.

Soil and water mixed to a thin paint and applied to the walls acts as a stain for up to two years; in other areas this might not be feasible, but at Lowry where the soil is a deep red, it works well. This technique helps to blend the newly stabilized areas with the prehistoric wall. A thicker slip of soil and water was painted over the cement joints of the west wall of Kiva A. The application of soil mortar to this wall would have taken many man-hours, because the bed of cement between the small building stones necessary to match the patch to the prehistoric was thin.

Definitions

Some of the more common definitions used in the following reports are listed below.

Capping - The upper 1-3 courses are removed and relaid with cement to protect the core of the wall against the weather. The number of courses relaid is dependent on the thickness of the building stones. Lancaster used a two-course cap at Lowry when he restored it in 1966-67. CU only capped one wall (Report 25).

Grouting - Cracks or large joints caused by crumbling prehistoric mortar are filled with a cement or soil mortar flush to the stone.

Pointing - Joints are cleared to a depth of 1.5-3cm, then filled with a soil mortar or soil cement to cover the new cement and blend the new areas with the prehistoric.

Spall - A chip of stone broken from a larger stone. Spalls were used at Lowry to push the mud back in the joints against the stone, and as levelers under building stones when a wall was being constructed.

Labor and Materials

A tabulation was kept of amounts of time used for different jobs at Lowry, to come up with useful data to figure time per contract. The tables are divided into the work associated with Kiva B (Appendix B), and the maintenance stabilization involved (Appendix C). All the tables briefly cover the area reconstructed, amount of cement used, other materials used, and the length of time (in man hours) to perform different jobs. The major work involved with Kiva B is also divided in the same manner, with the addition of excavation and building time.

Summary

Several facts are useful from this data: many factors other than the size of the reconstructed wall are involved in figuring the amount of time to repair a wall. The experience of the worker, the difficulty of the wall he is reconstructing, and the availability of building stones that do not require shaping appear to be the most important. If any excavation is necessary, the time is greatly increased as proved from the time spent reexcavating Kiva B. Data of this kind is generally useful but not exact, since the type of problem in every ruin is so different.

RUINS STABILIZATION RECORD   Report ___1___

Room ___12___

Kiva _____

RUIN __Lowry Ruin__

Personnel of party on this job: Wall (interior) _____

J.H., E.C.   (N,E,S,W) __East__

(Exterior) __x__

Floor, roof __No work was done on floor, roof.__

Reference to publications and justifications for job:

__Lowry Ruin in Southwestern Colorado;__ Paul S. Martin 1936
Field notes of Al Lancaster for 1966-67 Stabilization

Abutment joint with eastern wall of Rm. 14 is source of weakness in wall.
Wall has begun to slump at this point.

ARCHITECTURE

51 Orientation, plan and type (Situation, evidence of additional stories, period
of construction relative to surrounding rooms, evidence of burning, etc.)

Room 12 was built after Rm. 10 to the
west and before Rm. 14. Rms. 10 and 15
were built before Rms. 11, 12, or 14.

(For a more detailed map refer to Martin
1936, p. 197, Fig. 53)

Floor (Floor type: additional notes)

No work was done on floor.

Roof (Roof type: additional notes)

Not ascertainable.

Details (Notes on doorways, lintels, etc.)

Condition when work started: Report 1
Ancient Masonry:

Prehistoric soil mortar and spalls had washed out between building stones
leaving gaping joints. Building stones were still in line with courses showing
no slumping had occurred.

Repair or reconstruction previous to this work:

Reconstruction was done in 1966 by Al Lancaster and crew. The SE corner of
Rm. 12 was capped along with entire length of wall forming eastern boundaries
of Rm. 12 and Rm. 14. Capping itvolved the upper 2 courses. Portions of the
wall were rebuilt approx. 2 feet. All large joints were grouted with cement.

Materials, construction, and technique in making repairs or accomplishing job:

A patch of 7 courses was removed and reset with a mixture of Portland Type 1
and 11 cement and Shiprock sand. All newly cemented joints were pointed with
soil mortar containing 2 parts soil to 1 part sand.

Date work started: 8/23/74

Date work finished: 8/23/74

Man days of labor: 5 hrs. 30 min.

Larry V. Nordby   8/23/74

Archeologist-foreman   Date

a

b

Figure 34. Room 12, east exterior wall. a, northern portion of wall after stabilization; b, southern portion of wall after stabilization. No before photograph was taken; the wall can be seen in Fig. 35.

RUINS STABILIZATION RECORD   Report ___2___

A. E Ext. wall of Rm. 14
Room B. S Int. wall of Rm. 18
Kiva

RUIN ___Lowry Ruin___

Personnel of party on this job: Wall (Interior) ___ x (B)

JAA, NK   (N,E,S,W) ___(A)east and (B) south

(Exterior) ___ x (A)

Floor, roof ___

Report 2

Condition when work started:
Ancient Masonry:

A. The east exterior wall of Room 14 is capped on the upper 2 courses. The lower
courses are composed of prehistoric masonry. Stones beneath the capped area are
loose and the soil mortar is falling out and flaking off.

B. No prehistoric masonry remains in the area of patch on the South wall of Rm. 18.

Repair or reconstruction previous to this work:

References to publications and justifications for job:

Lowry Ruin in Southwestern Colorado; Paul S. Martin, 1936
Field notes of Al Lancaster for 1966-67 Stabilization

2 areas of Stabilization are covered in this report:
A. Erosion has occured in the eastern area of wall which was abutted
to NE corner of Room 12. Four to five courses in width by 1 m.
30 cm. in length require replacement.
B. A small patch was needed on S wall of Rm. 18

Reconstruction was done in 1956 by Al Lancaster. The top 2 courses of the
east wall of Room 14 were capped along with the south wall of Room 18. All
large joints were grouted with cement.

Materials, construction, and technique in making repairs or accomplishing job:

A. East Ext. wall of Room 14 - all loose stones were removed and reset with a
mixture of Portland cement and sand. The area reset was aprox. 4-5 courses
in height. Area was pointed with a soil mortar of 3 parts soil to 1 part
sand.
B. South Int. wall of Room 18 - several stones were reset with a mixture of
Portland cement and sand.

Date work started: A. 8/23/74   B. 9/5/74
Date work finished: A. 8/23/74   B. 9/5/74
Man days of labor: A. 7 hours, 30 min.   B. 1 hour

ARCHITECTURE

Orientation, plan and type (Situation, evidence of additional stories, period
of construction relative to surrounding rooms, evidence of burning, etc.)

A. Room 14 was built after surrounding
Rooms 15 and 18 and at the same time
as Rooms 12 and 16.
B. Room 18 was built before Rms. 14 and 16.

(For a more detailed map refer to Martin
1936, p. 199, Fig. 53)

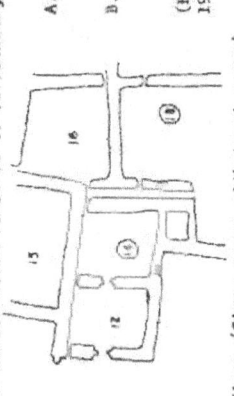

Floor (Floor type: additional notes)

No work was done on floor.

Roof (Roof type: additional notes)

Not ascertainable.

Details (Notes on doorways, lintels, etc.)

Larry V. Nordby   9/5/74
Archeologist-foreman   Date

53

a

b

Figure 35. Room 14, east exterior wall. a, several stones were
missing and large joints were created by crumbling mortar; wall
was slumping at the abuttment to Room 12; b, missing stones were
replaced and the wall was straightened.

Condition when work started:
Ancient Masonry:

A. Building stones had fallen in central area of wall from the 3rd to 8th courses. Soil mortar was in a crumbling state with stones loosened and several missing. Large joints were created by missing joints.

B. No prehistoric masonry remained, entire SE corner of this wall was set in cement in 1966.

Repair or reconstruction previous to this work:

Both areas were reconstructed in 1967 by Al Lancaster and crew by capping the upper 2 courses.

Materials, construction, and technique in making repairs or accomplishing job:

A. All loosened stones were removed along with all loose soil mortar. Stones were reset with a mixture of Portland Type I and II cement and Shiprock sand. All newly cemented joints were pointed with soil mortar of 2 parts soil to 1 part sand.

B. Loosened stones were reseted and reset with mixture of Portland cement and Shiprock sand. Area was pointed with soil mortar of 2 parts soil to 1 part sand.

Date work started: 8/23/74

Date work finished: 8/23/74

Man days of labor: A. 8 hours
B. 1 hour

Larry V. Notdby   8/23/74
Archeologist-foreman   Date

RUINS STABILIZATION RECORD   Report 3
Room
Kiva E

RUIN   Lowry Ruin

Personnel of party on this job: Wall (interior)   (N,E,S,W) south

A. DSK, JAL   (Exterior) x

B. JAL

Floor, roof   No work was done on floor, roof.

References to publications and justifications for job:

Lowry Ruin in Southwestern Colorado; Paul S. Martin, 1936
Field notes of Al Lancaster for 1966-67 stabilization

Two areas were worked on in this report. The 1st area is at the west end of Exterior south wall of Kiva E. This area needed a cement patch where wall was eroding beneath cement cap. The other area was at the east end of wall and required a patch of several stones.

ARCHITECTURE

Orientation, plan and type (Situation, evidence of additional stories, period of construction relative to surrounding rooms, evidence of burning, etc.)

A. This wall appears to have been built at the same time as Room 14 and Room 18 but the Martin is not clear on this.
B. This wall is not mentioned by Martin. It was possibly discovered later by Lancaster.

(For a more detailed map refer to Paul S Martin 1936, p. 197, Fig. 53)

Floor (Floor type: additional notes)

No work was done on floor.

Roof (Roof type: additional notes)

Not ascertainable.

Details (Notes on doorways, lintels, etc.)

a

b

Figure 36. Kiva E, south exterior wall. A, several stones were missing and large joints were created by crumbling mortar; b, stones were reset and all large joints were filled.

Figure 37. Kiva E, east exterior corner south of Kiva E.
View after corner was stabilized. Several stones were reset
and pointed with mortar.

RUINS STABILIZATION RECORD

Report 6
Room 21
Kiva

RUIN Lowry Ruin

Personnel of party on this job: Wall (interior) ___x___

    LFL, ASW   (N,E,S,W) __northwest corner__

            (Exterior) _____

         Floor, roof No work was done on the floor, roof.

References to publications and justifications for job:

Lowry Ruin in Southwestern Colorado: Paul S. Martin, 1936

Field notes of Al Lancaster for 1965-67 stabilization

Photograph taken before reconstruction shows area involved in erosion after
dirt was cleared from lower course of wall. Previous to being cleared this
corner showed severe cracking of concrete and loosened stones with several
areas showing stones completely missing.

ARCHITECTURE

Orientation, plan and type (Situation, evidence of additional stories, period
of construction relative to surrounding rooms, evidence of burning, etc.)

                            Room 21 is part of the original room block
                            of the ruin. Rooms 19, 21, 15, and 10
                            compose this room block and according to
                            Martin compose the earliest portion of ruin.
                            Rm. 16 and 22 were added in a later addition.

                            (For a more detailed map refer to Paul
                            Martin 1936, p. 197, Fig. 53)

Floor (Floor type: additional notes)

    No work was done on floor.

Roof (Roof type: additional notes)

    Not ascertainable.

Details (Notes on doorways, lintels, etc.)

    No work was done on doorways, etc.

Report 4

Condition when work started:
Ancient Masonry:

Corner of Rm. 21 showed cracking of soil mortar and concrete prior to
trench being dug along wall below soil level of room. The trench showed
intensive erosion had occurred in the portion of wall below soil level. A large
crack ran between the 5th and 6th course. Overall view of wall indicated wall
was slumped outward and downward.

Repair or reconstruction previous to this work:

Stabilization and rebuilding in 1966-67 by Al Lancaster. Portions of this
corner were reset with cement several courses lower than top two courses
which were capped. Rough walls were removed along west side of Rm. 21
along with a large amount of loose stone. Drainage is to the center of the
room.

Materials, construction, and technique in making repairs or accomplishing job:

Corner was stabilized by removing loose stones and soil mortar to a height
of 6 courses and resetting reused stone with a mixture of Portland Type I and
II cement and sand. Entire area cemented was pointed and spalled with a
mixture of soil mortar of 3 parts soil to 1 part sand.

Date work started: 8/23/74

Date work finished: 8/25/74

Man days of labor: 24 hours = 3 days

                           Larry V. Nordby   8/25/74
                           Archeologist-foreman   Date

a

b

Figure 38. Room 21, northwest interior corner. a, large area of
missing and fallen stones caused by undermining; b, stones were reset
and pointed with soil mortar, soil was banked against the wall and
sloped towards the center of the room.

c

d

Figure 38. Room 21, north interior wall. c, damage included fallen
stones and large joints; d, all loose stones were reset and large
joints were pointed with soil mortar.

RUINS STABILIZATION RECORD

Report _5_

Room _11_

Kiva _____

RUIN _Lowry Ruin_

Personnel of party on this job: Wall (Interior) __x__

(N,E,S,W) __West__

(Exterior) _____

Floor, roof _No work done on floor or roof._

References to publications and justifications for job:

Lowry Ruin in Southwestern Colorado; Paul S. Martin, 1936
Field notes of Al Lancaster for 1966-67 stabilization

Photograph taken before restoration shows eroding sandstone slabs with several missing in the middle area of wall. This wall is built of a different type of sandstone not common at this ruin.

ARCHITECTURE

Orientation, plan and type (Situation, evidence of additional stories, period of construction relative to surrounding rooms, evidence of burning, etc.)

Room 11 was built after Room 10 to the west but at the same time as surrounding Room 8 and 12.

(For more detailed map refer to Paul S. Martin 1936, p. 197, Fig. 53)

Floor (Floor type: additional notes)

No work was done on floor.

Roof (Roof type: additional notes)

None ascertainable.

Details (Notes on doorways, lintels, etc.)

No work done on doorways, etc.

Condition when work started:
Ancient Masonry:

Middle area of wall was eroded, soil mortar was flaking off in chunks with several stones in middle of wall completely missing.

Repair or reconstruction previous to this work:

Al Lancaster capped the upper two courses of this wall in 1966.

Materials, construction, and technique in making repairs or accomplishing job:

Loosened stone and eroding mortar was taken out of wall and stone was reused with mixture of Portland cement and Shiprock sand. A soil mortar mixture of three parts soil to one part sand was pointed into cement joints. Since this wall showed evidence of spalls prehistorically, spalls were pressed into joints of soil mortar to match up reconstructed wall to prehistoric wall.

Date work started: 8/24/74

Date work finished: 8/26/74

Man days of labor: 78½ hours = 2 days, 2 hours, 30 min.

_____   8/26/74
Larry V. Nordby   Date
Archeologist-foreman

Report 5

61

a

b

Figure 39. Room 11, west interior wall. a, several stones had
fallen from wall and stones of soft sandstone were eroding; b,
eroding and missing stones were replaced.

RUINS STABILIZATION RECORD

Report ___6___
Room _____
Kiva ___Great Kiva___

RUIN ___Lowry Ruin___

Personnel of party on this job: Wall (Interior) __x__

J.L.   (N,E,S,W) __West, East, and Northeast__

                                      (Exterior) _____

                          Floor, roof No work was done on floor or roof.

References to publications and justifications for job:

Lowry Ruin in Southwest Colorado; Paul S. Martin
Field Notes of Al Lancaster for 1966-67 stabilization

Photographs taken before stabilization show extent of damage in four different
areas. Three of these areas were small repair jobs of 3-3 stones which were
loosened or slipping from banquette wall. The other area involved the stairway.
The damage here was due to runoff from ground level into Kiva.

ARCHITECTURE

Orientation, plan and type (situation, evidence of additional stories, period
of construction relative to surrounding rooms, evidence of burning, etc.)

According to Paul S. Martin 1936 the
Great Kiva was built during the earliest
occupation.

[For more detailed map refer to Map 4,
Paul S. Martin 1936)

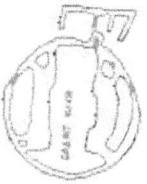

Floor (Floor type: additional notes)

No work was done on floor.

Roof (Roof type: additional notes)

Not ascertainable.

Details (Notes on doorways, lintels, etc.)

The main stairway into the Great Kiva was restored.

Condition when work started:
Ancient Masonry:

Prehistoric soil mortar was remaining in all areas which had eroded and needed
stabilization. The soil mortar was crumbling and falling out, creating large
joints between stones.

Repair or reconstruction previous to this work:

The Great Kiva was reconstructed in 1967 by Al Lancaster. A substantial amount
of stabilization was done. All fallen stones were replaced in the liner, wall
was brought to the surface and back repaired. All built in features, vaults,
column bases and rooms I, II, and III, north of Kiva were rebuilt. Moisture
was drained away from the top walls of Kiva. Wooden logs were replaced in the
steps and all large joints were grouted with cement.

Materials, construction, and technique in making repairs or accomplishing job:

Soil and sand was lowered into Great Kiva in buckets. Soil mortar was mixed
in Great Kiva then transported to small areas needing patches. A soil mortar
mixture of 2 parts soil to 1 part sand was used.

Date work started: 9/10/74

Date work finished: 9/10/74

Man days of labor: 6 hours

Larry V. Nordby   9/10/74

Archeologist-foreman   Date

Report 6

a

LOWRY
GREAT KIVA
STAIRWAY

b

Figure 40. Great Kiva, stairway. a, stairway before stabilization
in 1966; b, water runoff down stairway caused erosion behind wooden
post steps.

c

Figure 40. Great Kiva, stairway. c, stones behind wooden post steps were reset.

a

b

Figure 41. Great Kiva, northeast bench. a, mortar eroded beneath cement cap leaving large joints; b, all joints were grouted with soil mortar.

a

b

Figure 42. Great Kiva, east bench. a, mortar eroded beneath
cement cap leaving large joints; b, all joints were grouted
with soil mortar.

a

b

Figure 43. Great Kiva, west bench. a, one building stone was missing from bench wall; b, stone was reset and large joints were grouted.

Report ____7____

Room ___16___

Kiva _____

RUIN ___Lowry Ruin___

Personnel of party on this job: Wall (Interior) ___x___ (N,E,S,W) ___South___ (Exterior) _____

JAL took loose stones from wall and put in temporary support. EGA and SK did stone work. CRM and JAH grouted cement joints with sand mortar. Floor, roof ___No work was done on floor, roof.___

References to publications and justifications for job:

Lowry Ruin in Southwestern Colorado; Paul S. Martin 1936
Field notes of Al Lancaster for 1966-67 Stabilization

Several different photographic views were taken of the damage to this wall to illustrate how extensive it was. The bulge in this wall was evident in 1967 but was not repaired at that time because damage was not as extensive. Since 1967, bulge has increased providing justification for extensive stone work; wall was considered unsafe.

ARCHITECTURE

Orientation, plan and type (Situation, evidence of additional stories, period of construction relative to surrounding rooms, evidence of burning, etc.)

Rm. 16 was built after Rms. 15 and 21. Other surrounding rooms 22, 23, 24, 18 and 14 were built during the same time period as Rm. 16.

(For a more detailed map refer to Paul S. Martin 1936, p. 197, Fig. 53)

Floor (Floor type: additional notes)

No work was done on floor.

Roof (Roof type: additional notes)

Not uncertainable.

Details (Notes on doorways, lintels, etc.)

No work was done.

69

Condition when work started:
Ancient Masonry:

The area involving major restoration in the wall involved prehistoric mortar. A bulge occurred in the central area of S interior wall of Rm. 16 possible prehistorically after abandonment. It became worn after wall was capped in 1967. Also below bulged area are multiple cracks resulting from the stress of a superior separation of wall.

Repair or reconstruction previous to this work:

This wall was reconstructed in 1967 by Al Lancaster. At that time it was noted that the wall had an extensive bulge in the central area of the S interior wall. However the decision was made to cap top three courses and to leave bulge as it was. Other restoration of this wall involved large joints being grouted with cement.

Materials, construction, and technique in making repairs or accomplishing job:

Extensive bulge was removed along with all loose soil mortar. A wooden prop of 2 x 4 boards was put in wall to support upper 2-3 courses after removal of damaged portion of wall. Three sections of rebar were placed within wall oriented E-W. These were placed within wall to reduce possibility of future lateral separation. Wooden supports were left in wall when stones were relaid with cement. Wall was stepped in from the lower courses to upper courses to decrease bulge. The bulge was not entirely removed. All newly cemented areas and large joints were pointed with soil mortar.

Date work started: 8/31/74

Date work finished: 9/2/74

Man days of labor: 168 hrs. - 21 days

_____Larry V. Nordby_____ ___9/2/74___
Archeologist-foreman   Date

a

b

Figure 44. Room 16, south interior wall. a, lateral seperation caused wall to bulge outward; b, view of exterior side of wall shows that damage did not extend through the thickness of the wall.

c

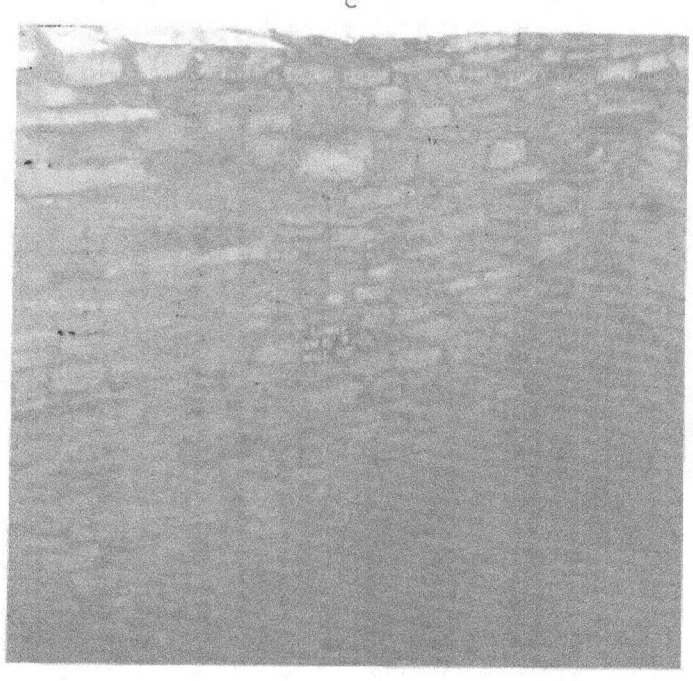

d

Figure 44. Room 16, south interior wall. c, wooden prop placed in the wall to support upper 2-3 courses after removal of the damaged portion; d, south view of wall after stabilization.

RUINS STABILIZATION RECORD   Report _____8_____

                                    Room __14__

                                    Kiva _____

RUIN __Lowry Ruin__

Personnel of party on this job: Wall (Interior) _____

        LVN   (N,E,S,W) __South__

                     (Exterior) __S exterior entrance__

                Floor, roof __No work was done on floor, roof.__

References to publications and justifications for job:

__Lowry Ruin in Southwestern Colorado; Paul S. Martin 1936__
__Field notes of Al Lancaster on 1966-67 Stabilization__

Several small building stones had slipped from wall weakening wall and
creating an area where extensive damage could occur.

ARCHITECTURE

Orientation, plan and type (Situation, evidence of additional stories, period
of construction relative to surrounding rooms, evidence of burning, etc.)

Rms. 12 and 14 were built during the same
time period as Rms. 16 and 18. Rms 10
and 15 were built in an earlier period.

(For more detailed map refer to Paul
S. Martin 1936, p. 197, Fig. 53)

Floor (Floor type: additional notes)

        No work was done.

Roof (Roof type: additional notes)

        Not ascertainable.

Details (Notes on doorways, lintels, etc.)

        When the doorway was stabilized in 1966, it was only restored to
        two courses above bench of T-shaped doorway.

72

Condition when work started:
Ancient Masonry:

Beneath the upper two course cement cap the original prehistoric wall still
existed intact. This wall was primarily in good condition except for one building
stone missing from East side of doorway and large joints which needed grouting.

Repair or reconstruction previous to this work:

This wall was restored and stabilized in 1966 by Al Lancaster. The upper two
courses of wall was capped with cement and all large joints were grouted
with cement.

Materials, construction, and technique in making repairs or accomplishing job:

Old building stones were used to relay stones which were missing or were
loosened. Stones were reset with a mixture of Portland Type I and II cement and
Shiprock sand. Newly cemented joints and other large joints were pointed with
a soil mortar mixture of three parts soil to 1 part sand.

Date work started: 8/26/74

Date work finished: 8/26/74

Man days of labor: 4 hrs.

                                    Larry V. Nordby   8/26/74
                                    Archeologist-foreman   Date

a

b

Figure 45. Room 14, south exterior entrance. a, stones were missing from both sides of the entrance and mortar was loose and cracking; b, after stones were reset and joints grouted.

RUINS STABILIZATION RECORD

Report ___9___

Room ___13___

Kiva _____

RUIN ___Lowry Ruin___

Personnel of party on this job: Wall (Interior) _____

J.H.   (N,E,S,W) ___South___

                        (Exterior) ___Entrance way___

Floor, roof __No work was done on floor, roof.__

References to publications and justifications for job:

Lowry Ruin in Southwestern Colorado; Paul S. Martin, 1936
Field notes of Al Lancaster for 1966-67 stabilization

Large cracks were occurring in prehistoric mortar and masonry creating loose
stones which eventually slipped from wall leaving gaps between stones. Cracks
and gaps needed to be repaired in order to stop erosion of entire wall.

ARCHITECTURE

Orientation, plan and type (situation, evidence of additional stories, period
of construction relative to surrounding rooms, evidence of burning, etc.)

Rms. 12 was built during the same time
period as Rms. 11 and 14. Rms. 10 and
15 were built in the period previous to
this which was the earliest building
phase at Lowry.

(For a more detailed map refer to Paul
S. Martin 1936, p. 197, Fig. 53)

Floor (Floor type: additional notes)

No work was done on floor.

Roof (Roof type: additional notes)

Not ascertainable.

Details (Notes on doorways, lintels, etc.)

This entranceway was first restored in 1965. It was restored to
several courses above bench level of T doorway.

Report 9

Condition when work started:
Ancient Masonry:

The entranceway was composed primarily of prehistoric masonry excluding
upper two courses of wall which are capped and small areas which were grouted
with cement. The prehistoric masonry was cracking in many areas with large
chinks of mortar falling from between stones causing a general loosening of
courses. Several building stones were missing leaving large gaps in walls.

Repair or reconstruction previous to this work:

The South wall of Room 13 was capped in 1966 by Al Lancaster. All large joints
in the wall were also grouted with cement.

Materials, construction, and technique in making repairs or accomplishing job:

Entranceway was restored by removing all loose stones and replacing these along
with those that were completely missing. Building stones were reset with a
mixture of Portland Type I and II cement and Shiprock sand. All of the newly
cemented area and areas involving large joints were pointed with mortar. The
soil mortar was composed of two parts soil to 1 part sand.

Date work started: 8/26/74

Date work finished: 8/27/74

Man days of labor: 12 hours, 35 min.=1day, 4 hrs., 35 min.

Larry V. Nordby   8/27/74
Archeologist-foreman   Date

74

a

b

Figure 46. Room 12, south exterior entrance. a, large joints
resulted from erosion of mortar; b, joints were grouted with cement.

RUINS STABILIZATION RECORD   Report ___10___

Room ___31___

Kiva _____

RUIN ___Lowry Ruin___

Personnel of party on this job: Wall (interior) _x_

                      (N,E,S,W) __East__

JAH, ASH   (Exterior) _____

             Floor, roof _No work was done on floor or roof._

References to publications and justifications for job:

Lowry Ruin in Southwestern Colorado; Paul S. Martin, 1936
Field notes of Al Lancaster for 1966-67 stabilization

Immediate stabilization of this wall was needed before erosion occurred,
completely undermining the wall as a result.

ARCHITECTURE

Orientation, plan and type (Situation, evidence of additional stories, period
of construction relative to surrounding rooms, evidence of burning, etc.)

Rm. 31 was built during the last building
phase of Lowry. Surrounding Rms. 9,32,
37, and 36 were built during the same time
period. Kiva A and Rm. 27 were built
earlier.

(For a more detailed map refer to Paul
S. Martin 1936, p. 197-198, Fig. 53)

Floor (Floor type: additional notes)

No work was done on floor.

Roof (Roof type: additional notes)

Not uncertainable.

Details (Notes on doorways, lintels, etc.)

Condition when work started:
Ancient Masonry:

The upper two courses of wall was capped with cement. The damage to wall began
below cement cap. The prehistoric wall was undermined by water flowing off the
tops of walls and drainage from the surface of the room. The extent of damage
involved 4-5 courses. In most areas the building stones were missing above
the surface and dislodged from wall or loose below surface.

Repair or reconstruction previous to this work:

Al Lancaster capped the upper two courses of this wall in 1966. Extensive
stabilization was done in other areas of Rm. 31. The west wall was almost
completely rebuilt. The South wall was rebuilt aprox. two feet. The North
wall was raised as a brace for leaning wall on the West. All walls were
capped and loose stone and dirt was removed with drainage to the center of
room.

Materials, construction, and technique in making repairs or accomplishing job:

A trench was first dug in front of interior east wall of room 31 to locate the
extent of undermining to the wall. A gap of 2-3 courses was observed below
surface level of room, the length of erosion was from NE corner to 1 meter
from SE corner. Old building stones were reset in eroded area with a mixture
of Portland Type I and II cement and Shiprock sand. Area was pointed with a
soil mortar mixture of three parts soil to 1 part sand.

Date work started: 8/26/74

Date work finished: 8/27/74

Man days of labor: 15 hrs = 1 day, 7 hrs.

_____ _Larry V. Nordby_ _8/27/74_
                   Archeologist-foreman   Date

Figure 47. Room 31, east interior wall. Wall was undermined 2-3
courses beneath upper 2 course cement cap. No photo was taken
before stabilization.

RUINS STABILIZATION RECORD

Room 8

Kiva

RUIN   Lowry Ruin

Personnel of party on this job: Wall (Interior) X

JAL gave demonstration to NK.   (N,E,S,W) East, South

(Exterior) X

Floor, roof No work was done on floor or roof.

References to publications and justifications for job:

Lowry Ruin in Southwestern Colorado; Paul S. Martin, 1936
Field notes of Al Lancaster for 1966-67 stabilization

a) E entrance to Rm. 8: Mud mortar was crumbling and flaking around lintel and small windows located to the N and S of entrance. Also wall joints showed large gaps where soil mortar had fallen out.
b) S interior wall of Rm. 8: Four small windows or shelves line this wall. Soil mortar was crumbling out of the interior and above lintels.

ARCHITECTURE

Orientation, plan and type (Situation, evidence of additional stories, period of construction relative to surrounding rooms, evidence of burning, etc.)

Room 8 was built after Room 10 and during the same time period as other surrounding Rms. 11, 12, 20.

(For more detailed map refer to Paul S. Martin, 1936)

Floor (Floor type: additional notes)

No work was done on floor.

Roof (Roof type: additional notes)

Not ascertainable.

Details (Notes on doorways, lintels, etc.)

Prehistoric mortar was crumbling above E entrance and above all windows on this wall and S wall of Room 8.

Condition when work started:
Ancient Masonry:

Spalling and mortar was crumbling around doorway and lintels. Windows or niches within Rm. 8 (S int. wall) had loose prehistoric mortar falling out and dislodged building stones. Lintels above these niches were loosened and needed grouting with soil mortar.

Repair or reconstruction previous to this work:

Al Lancaster stabilized and rebuilt Rm. 8 in 1966-67. The West wall was rebuilt 2-3 feet. The South wall was built up about 3 feet in center. Four large niches or windows were repaired and new lintels put in. On the East wall new lintels were put over the doorway and one window. East wall was rebuilt about 14" above doorway. The East end of N wall was built up about 2 feet. Holes were grouted in the W end of the N wall. All walls were capped with the large joints grouted.

Materials, construction, and technique in making repairs or accomplishing job:

a) 3:1 proportions of soil to sand was used to point entrance to Rm. 8 over lintel and N wall of entrance wall. A 2:1 proportion of soil mortar was used on Ext. entrance wall 5 of entrance.
b) Old stone with a mixture of Rockmont Type I cement was used to reset stones in windows on S int. wall of Rm. 8. Area surrounding windows was pointed with a mixture of mortar of three parts soil to 1 part sand.

Date work started: 8/24/74

Date work finished: 8/26/74

Man days of labor: 7 hrs., 45 min.

Larry V. Nordby   8/26/74
Archeologist-foreman   Date

Figure 48. Room 8, east exterior entrance. All large joints of the interior and exterior wall were grouted. No photo was taken before stabilization.

RUINS STABILIZATION RECORD   Report ___12___

                                    Room ___33___

                                    Kiva _____

RUIN Lowry Ruin

Personnel of party on this job: Wall (interior)   x

                                (N,E,S,W) West

                                (Exterior) _____

                    Floor, roof No work was done on floor or roof.

ASW,KL,DK

References to publications and justifications for job:

Lowry Ruin in Southwestern Colorado; Paul S. Martin, 1936
Field notes of Al Lancaster for 1966-67 stabilization.

ARCHITECTURE

Orientation, plan and type (Situation, evidence of additional stories, period
of construction relative to surrounding rooms, evidence of burning, etc.)

Rm. 33 was built after Rooms 17 and 13
but during the same time period as Rms.
32, 35, and 34.

(For more detailed map refer to Paul
S. Martin 1936, p. 196, Fig. 54)

Floor (Floor type: additional notes)

No work was done on floor.

Roof (Roof type: additional notes)

Not ascertainable.

Details (Notes on doorways, lintels, etc.)

80

Condition when work started:
Ancient Masonry:

Deep gaps were apparent between building stones where original prehistoric
mortar had eroded out of wall.

Repair or reconstruction previous to this work:

The upper two courses were capped in 1966 by Al Lancaster.

Materials, construction, and technique in making repairs or accomplishing job:

Pointing and replacing of spalls was limited to lower nine courses of wall.
The entire length of wall N-S was pointed. A soil mortar of two parts soil
to 1 part sand was used for pointing.

Date work started: 8/28/74

Date work finished: 8/28/74

Man days of labor: 12 hrs. = 1 day, 4 hrs.

_____
Larry V. Nordby   8/28/74
Archeologist-foreman   Date

a

b

Figure 49. Room 33, north end of west interior wall. a, damage
was confined to mortar crumbling from joints; excavation below
ground surface showed no undermining of wall; b, soil mortar and
spalls were replaced in the lower portion of the wall.

81

c

d

Figure 49. Room 33, south end of the west interior wall. c, damage
was confined to mortar crumbling from joints; excavation below
ground surface showed no undermining of wall; b, soil mortar and
spalls were replaced in the lower portion of the wall.

82

RUINS STABILIZATION RECORD

Report 13
3 areas worked:
A. Ent. to Room 11
B. E Ent. to Room 10
C. Small patches to Room 10

Room _____

Kiva _____

RUIN Lowry Ruin

Personnel of party on this job: Wall (Interior) ___ x (N,E,S,W) East and west (Rm. 10), North (Rm. 11)

(Exterior) ___ x

Floor, roof No work done on floor or roofs.

KL - A. N Ent. to Room 11
B. E Ent. to Room 10

W. - C. 2 small patches of W wall of Room 10

Condition when work started:
Ancient Masonry:

Only two areas covered in this record still contained prehistoric mortar. These areas were the patch areas in Room 10 and the one small area on N Exterior wall of Room 11. In both areas mud mortar and several building stones had fallen out of wall.

References to publications and justifications for job:

Lowry Ruin In Southwestern Colorado; Paul S. Martin, 1936
Field notes of Al Lancaster for 1966-67 stabilization

A. N Ent. to Rm. 11 - Building stones composing step into Room 11 were loose from cement (1966-67 Al Lancaster) and small area W of Ent. had gaping hole where one stone had fallen out.
B. E Entrance to Rm. 10 - Large building stone composing S end of 1st upper course of bench portion of T doorway was missing.
C. Several small patches were made on the W lat. wall of Room 10 where bldg. stones were dislodged from wall.

Repair or reconstruction previous to this work:

A. North Ent. to Room 11 was rebuilt in 1966-67 by Al Lancaster and reset in cement immediately surrounding Ent. In area of small patch W of Ent. no stabilization had previously been done.
B. East Ent. to Room 10 was also stabilized by Al Lancaster in 1966-67 in the same manner as N Ent. to Room 11 (this doorway and one in west wall were stabilized by Ben Wilford while excavation was in progress)
C. No previous stabilization.

ARCHITECTURE

Orientation, plan and type (Situation, evidence of additional stories, period of construction relative to surrounding rooms, evidence of burning, etc.)

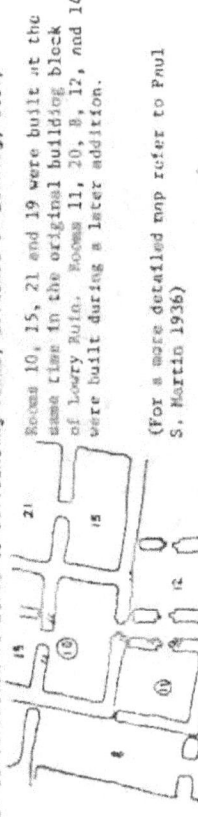

Rooms 10, 15, 21 and 19 were built at the same time in the original building block of Lowry Ruin. Rooms 11, 20, 8, 12, and 14 were built during a later addition.

(For a more detailed map refer to Paul S. Martin 1936)

Materials, construction, and technique in making repairs or accomplishing job:

A. North Ent. to Room 11 - Old stone was reused with a mixture of Shiprock sand and Portland Type I cement. A soil mortar mixture of 2 parts soil to 1 part sand was used to point up newly cemented areas.
B. E Ent. to Room 10 - Old stone was reshaped and reused with a mixture of Shiprock sand and Portland Type I cement. A soil mortar mixture of two parts soil to 1 part sand was used to point up newly cemented areas.
C. Small patches in Room 10 were stabilized with small amounts of cement and large chunk type spalls. A soil mortar mixture of three parts soil to one part sand was used to point up newly cemented areas.

Floor (Floor type: additional notes)

No work was done on floors in any of the 3 areas in this report.

Roof (Roof type: additional notes)

Not ascertainable.

Date work started: 8/31/74

Date work finished: 8/31/74

Man days of labor: 6 hours, 10 min.

Details (Notes on doorways, lintels, etc.)

A. N Ent. to Rm. 11 - stones composing step were reset in cement then mudded.
B. E Ent. to Room 10 - stones composing bench of S end were reset and replaced.

Larry V. Nordby _____ 8/31/74
Archeologist-foreman _____ Date

83

a

b

Figure 50. Room 11, north exterior entrance. a, step was loose,
a stone was missing from the west side of the entrance and mortar
was cracking from the joints; b, after stabilization.

Figure 51. Room 10, exterior entrance. Several stones were replaced on the top course of the south bench of the T-doorway. No photo was taken before stabilization.

Condition when work started:
Ancient Masonry:

Several courses on the surface level had building stones which were loosened from prehistoric mortar. In the general area below offset in wall large joints were evident between building stones where prehistoric mortar was crumbling out of wall.

Repair or reconstruction previous to this work:

This wall was stabilized and reconstructed in 1966. The top portion of wall had fallen leaving wall slightly bowed. When the wall was rebuilt the bottom portion of the wall was offset in order to tie the upper portion of the wall to the bottom portion. This offset was the portion of wall that needed stabilization in 1974.

Materials, construction, and technique in making repairs or accomplishing job:

In the original stabilization in 1966 when this wall was offset an unstable condition developed due to the high ground surface of the area to the North. A small hole developed in the wall in the area of the offset. This hole was enlarged into a drainage hole to drain off water to the North which had been excavated in 1974. All loose stones were removed from the wall and reset with a mixture of Portland Type I and II cement and Shiprock sand.

Date work started: 9/9/74

Date work finished: 9/9/74

Man days of labor: 6 hours

Larry V. Nordby   9/9/74
Archeologist-foreman   Date

RUINS STABILIZATION RECORD

Report ___14___
Room ___27___
Kiva _____

RUIN   Lowry Ruin

Personnel of party on this job: Wall (interior) ___x___

JAL   (N,E,S,W) North

          (Exterior) _____

          Floor, roof   No work was done on floor or roof.

References to publications and justifications for job:

Lowry Ruin in Southwestern Colorado; Paul S. Martin, 1936
Field notes of Al Lancaster for 1966-67 stabilization.

The N wall of Room 27 was being undermined by the loosening of stones and crumbling of soil mortar beneath areas laid in cement.

ARCHITECTURE

Orientation, plan and type (Situation, evidence of additional stories, period of construction relative to surrounding rooms, evidence of burning, etc.)

Room 27 was built during the same time period as Kiva B. Other surrounding Rms. 9, 31, 37 and Kiva H were built during a later period.

(For a more detailed map refer to Paul S. Martin 1936, p. 196, Fig. 53)

Floor (Floor type: additional notes)

No work was done on floor.

Roof (Roof type: additional notes)

Not ascertainable.

Details (Notes on doorways, lintels, etc.)

a

b

Figure 52. Room 27, north interior wall. a, several stones were missing and the mortar was crumbling beneath cement cap; b, stones were reset and the joints were grouted.

RUINS STABILIZATION RECORD

Report ___15___
Room ___23___
Kiva _____

RUIN ___Lowry Ruin___

Personnel of party on this job: Wall (Interior) ___x___

(N,E,S,W) ___East, and north___

(Exterior) _____

Floor, roof ___No work was done on floor, roof.___

References to publications and justifications for job:

Lowry Ruin in Southwestern Colorado; Paul S. Martin, 1936
Field Notes of Al Lancaster for 1966-67 Stabilization

Cement patches were necessary on the interior east and north walls of Rm. 23 to stop erosion before a larger area was involved.

ARCHITECTURE

Orientation, plan and type (Situation, evidence of additional stories, period of construction relative to surrounding rooms, evidence of burning, etc.)

Rm. 23 was built during the same time as surrounding Rms. 22, 16, and 24.

(For more detailed map refer to Paul S. Martin 1936, Fig. 53)

Floor (Floor type: additional notes)

No work was done of floor.

Roof (Roof type: additional notes)

Not ascertainable.

Details (Notes on doorways, lintels, etc.)

Report 15

Condition when work started:
Ancient Masonry:

Prehistoric masonry was still present beneath upper two course cement cap; this is where the erosion occurred. The area eroding out was aprox. 130 cm. in length and extended for 5-6 courses below upper cement cap. A small area on the north wall contained an area where a large joint was created by the crumbling of soil mortar. This joint was grouted with cement.

Repair or reconstruction previous to this work:

This wall was stabilized in 1967 by Al Lancaster. All walls were capped with two courses and more in some areas. The northwest corner was rebuilt from the floor up.

Materials, construction, and technique in making repairs or accomplishing job:

The area on the east wall below cement cap was cleaned out with all loose building stones and mortar removed. These stones were reset with a mixture of Portland Type I and II cement and Shiprock sand. All newly cemented joints were pointed with a soil mortar mixture of three parts soil to one part sand. A large joint on the north wall was grouted with cement.

Date work started: 8/4/74

Date work finished: 8/5/74

Man days of labor: 6 hours, 15 min.

Larry V. Nordby ___8/5/74___
Archeologist-foreman   Date

88

a

b

Figure 53. Room 23, east interior wall. a, masonry immediately beneath the cap was eroding; b, view after stabilization; photo board is mislabeled.

a

b

Figure 54. Room 23, north interior wall. a, several areas of the
wall had large gaps resulting from crumbling mortar; b, after
stabilization; Photo board is mislabeled.

RUINS STABILIZATION RECORD

Report _____16_____

Room _unnumbered space E of Kiva B_

Kiva _____

RUIN _____Lowry Ruin_____

Personnel of party on this job: Wall (Interior) ___x___

JAH   (N,E,S,W) ___East___

         (Exterior) _____

Floor, roof _No work was done on floor, roof._

References to publications and justifications for job:

Lowry Ruin in Southwestern Colorado; Paul S. Martin, 1936
Field notes of Al Lancaster for 1946-67 stabilization

Wall was being undermined by water beneath cement cap creating an unstable
condition for entire wall.

ARCHITECTURE

**Orientation, plan and type (Situation, evidence of additional stories, period
of construction relative to surrounding rooms, evidence of burning, etc.)**

This space was formed with the building
of Kiva A and Kiva B. Rms. 27 and 17
were built during the same time period.
Rms. 31, 32, and 33 were built during a
later period.

(For a more detailed map refer to Paul
S. Martin, 1936)

Floor (Floor type: additional notes)

No work was done on floor.

Roof (Roof type: additional notes)

Not ascertainable.

Details (Notes on doorways, lintels, etc.)

91

Condition when work started:
Ancient Masonry:

A cap of four courses was rebuilt in 1946. The area of erosion was below this
cap where prehistoric masonry is still present. A portion of the original
veneer was eroding from wall. The prehistoric soil mortar was soft and crumbling
out in chunks. Along with veneer a new foundation had to be rebuilt for wall
since stones were loose at the base of wall.

Repair or reconstruction previous to this work:

The walls of this room were capped in 1946 by Al Lancaster. The area involving
1974 stabilization had not been excavated in 1946.

Materials, construction, and technique in making repairs or accomplishing job:

All loose stones were removed along with cracking soil mortar. Building
stones were reset in veneer and at the base of wall with a mixture of Portland
Type I and II and Shiprock sand.

Date work started: 9/9/74

Date work finished: 9/10/74

Man days of labor: 6 hrs.

Larry V. Nordby   9/10/74

_____Archeologist-foreman_____   _Date_

a

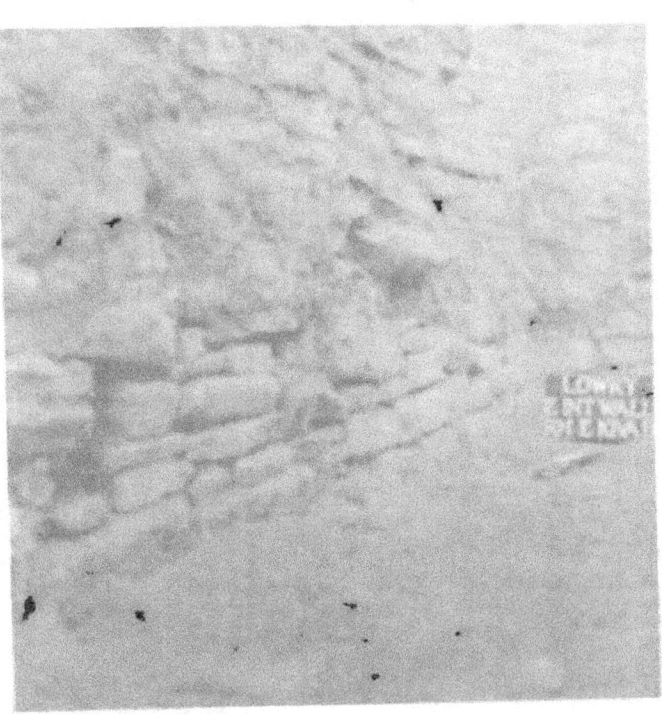

b

Figure 55. Space east of Kiva B (unnumbered), east interior wall.
a, wall was undermined in large area; b, missing and loosened stones
were reset.

RUINS STABILIZATION RECORD

Report _____ 17 _____

Room _____

Kiva B (NE portion of upper wall)

RUIN   Lowry Ruin

Personnel of party on this job: Wall (Interior)   x

ASW, CWM   (N,E,S,W) Northeast

                            (Exterior) _____

                    Floor, roof No work was done on floor, roof.

References to publications and justifications for job:

Lowry Ruin in Southwestern Colorado; Paul S. Martin, 1936
Field notes of Al Lancaster for 1966-67 stabilization

There were several justifications for stabilizing this wall. The wall was
dangerous to people working in Kiva B. A stable base was needed in order to
place a temporary roof over Kiva B.

ARCHITECTURE

Orientation, plan and type (Situation, evidence of additional stories, period
of construction relative to surrounding rooms, evidence of burning, etc.)

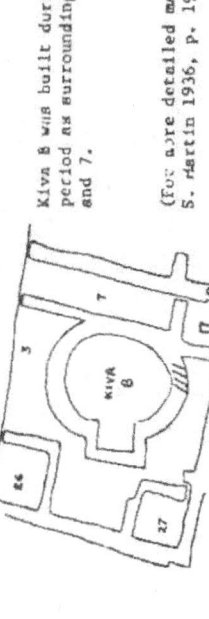

Kiva B was built during the same time
period as surrounding Rms. 26, 27, 3,
and 7.

(For a more detailed map refer to Paul
S. Martin 1936, p. 197, Fig. 53)

Floor (Floor type: additional notes)

    No work was done on floor.

Roof (Roof type: additional notes)

    Not ascertainable.

Details (Notes on doorways, lintels, etc.)

93

Report 17

Condition when work started:

Ancient Masonry:

The wall contained no previous stabilization therfore entire wall was prehistoric.
The wall was unstable with loose building stones and crumbling mortar from top
course to 6-7 courses beneath. The entire thickness of wall had to be rebuilt.

Repair or reconstruction previous to this work:

No reconstruction was done prior to this time. Kiva B was partially excavated
in 1933-34 by Paul S. Martin and was immediately backfilled to preserve as
much as possible.

Materials, construction, and technique in making repairs or accomplishing job:

The entire thickness of wall was taken down 6-7 courses. All loose stones and
crumbling of loose mortar was taken out. Building stones were reset with a
mixture of Portland Type I and II cement and Shiprock sand. All cemented
joints were pointed with a soil mortar mixture of four parts soil to one part
sand.

Date work started: 8/3/74

Date work finished: 8/4/74

Man days of labor: 36 hrs. = 4 days, 4 hrs.

                    Larry V. Nordby   8/4/74

                    Archaeologist-foreman   Date

a

b

Figure 56. Kiva B, northeast wall. a, stones were loosened through-
out the thickness of the wall; b, wall was rebuilt to an even level
to provide a foundation for roof.

Room ___24___
Kiva _____

RUIN ___Lowry Ruin___

Personnel of party on this job: Wall (interior) ___X___
    (N,E,S,W) ___South___
    (Exterior) _____
    Floor, roof ___No work was done on floor, roof.___

    JAU, JAM

References to publications and justifications for job:

Lowry Ruin in Southwestern Colorado; Paul S. Martin, 1936
Field notes of Al Lancaster for 1966-67 stabilization

Erosion of several courses beneath cap of wall created an unsafe condition since wall is often travelled on by visitors to Lowry.

ARCHITECTURE

Orientation, plan and type (Situation, evidence of additional stories, period of construction relative to surrounding rooms, evidence of burning, etc.)

Room 24 was built during the same time period as all surrounding rooms excluding Rm. 18 which was built before Room 24 during the first building phase.

(For more detailed map refer to Martin 1936, Fig. 53, p. 196)

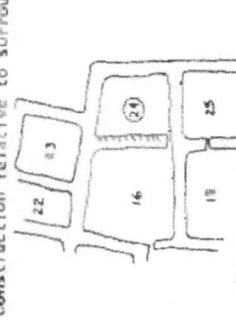

Floor (Floor type: additional notes)

No work was done on floor.

Roof (Roof type: additional notes)

Not ascertainable.

Details (Notes on doorways, lintels, etc.)

95

Condition when work started:
Ancient Masonry:

Prehistoric masonry of 2-3 courses beneath 2 course cement cap have bulged outward. Building stones and mud mortar are loose in some areas and missing in other areas. The area needing stabilized extends the entire length of wall in a E-W direction.

Repair or reconstruction previous to this work:

Al Lancaster capped this wall in 1967 after excavating Room for the first time.

Materials, construction, and technique in making repairs or accomplishing job:

Building stones and soil mortar was removed from wall beneath top 2 course cap. Stones were reset with a mixture of Portland Type I and II cement and Shiprock sand. All newly cemented joints were pointed with a mixture of soil mortar of two parts soil to one part sand.

Date work started: 9/3/74

Date work finished: 9/4/74

Man days of labor: 18 hrs. = 2 days, 2 hrs.

Larry V. Nordby   9/4/74
Archeologist-foreman   Date

Figure 57. Room 24, south interior wall. Replaced 2-3 courses
immediately below the cement cap. No photo was taken before
stabilization.

Condition when work started:
Ancient Masonry:

Only a small portion of prehistoric masonry remained in the entrance. This was several courses of stone to the north and south of doorway just above ground surface level. In this case the stones were loose in areas still containing prehistoric mortar.

Repair or reconstruction previous to this work:

This entrance was restored and stabilized in 1966-67 by Al Lancaster. The center of the east wall (over and to either side of doorway) was almost half rebuilt. Lintels were replaced over doorway.

Materials, construction, and technique in making repairs or accomplishing job:

All loose stones were removed and prehistoric soil mortar and cement was chiseled out of wall. Building stones were reset with a mixture of Portland Type I and II cement and Shiprock sand. All newly cemented joints were pointed with a soil mortar mixture of 3 parts soil to 1 part sand.

Date work started: 8/4/74
Date work finished: 8/5/74
Man days of labor: 9 hrs., 20 min. = 1 day, 1 hr., 20 min.

Larry V. Nordby   8/5/74
Archaeologist-foreman   Date

RUINS STABILIZATION RECORD   Report 19
Room 21
Kiva _____

RUIN Lowry Ruin

Personnel of party on this job: Wall (Interior) _____ x
(N,E,S,W) East
(Exterior) _____
ECA

Floor, roof No work was done on floor, roof.

References to publications and justifications for job:

Lowry Ruin in Southwestern Colorado; Paul S. Martin, 1936
Field notes of Al Lancaster for 1966-67 stabilization

This wall was stabilized in 1967 but the wall settled causing the entrance to crack. Another cause for cracking was water seepage from associated Room 15 to the east which has a higher ground surface than Room 21. A hole possibly caused by a rodent was evident through entrance up to ground surface of Room 15.

ARCHITECTURE

Orientation, plan and type (Situation, evidence of additional stories, period of construction relative to surrounding rooms, evidence of burning, etc.)

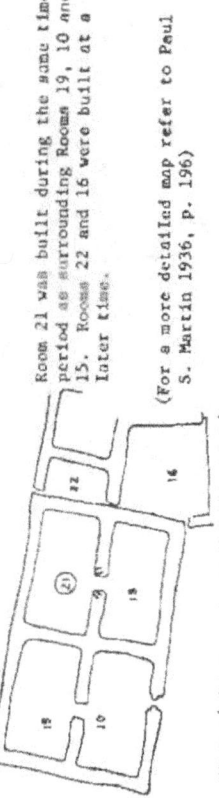

Room 21 was built during the same time period as surrounding Rooms 19, 10 and 15. Rooms 22 and 16 were built at a later time.

(For a more detailed map refer to Paul S. Martin 1936, p. 196)

Floor (Floor type: additional notes)

No work was done on floor.

Roof (Roof type: additional notes)

Not ascertainable.

Details (Notes on doorways, lintels, etc.)

Lintels of E entrance to Room 21 were replaced in 1967 by Al Lancaster.

a

b

Figure 58. Room 21, east interior entrance. a, before stabilization in 1966; b, rodent hole on exterior side that probably caused damage to the interior side.

c

d

Figure 58. Room 21, east interior entrance. c, a large crack
extended from the lintel to ground surface and stones were loose
to either side of the entrance; d, after stabilization.

RUINS STABILIZATION RECORD

Report ___20___

Room ___4___

Kiva _____

RUIN ___Lowry Ruin___

Personnel of party on this job: Wall (Interior) ___x___

(N,E,S,W) ___SE corner___

(Exterior) _____

Floor, roof ___No work done on floor, roof.___

References to publications and justifications for job:

Lowry Ruin in Southwestern Colorado; Paul S. Martin, 1936
Field notes of Al Lancaster for 1966-67

Several building stones had slipped from wall leaving gaps and the inner core of wall open to erosion.

ARCHITECTURE

Orientation, plan and type (Situation, evidence of additional stories, period of construction relative to surrounding rooms, evidence of burning, etc.)

Room 4 was built during the same time period as all surrounding rooms.

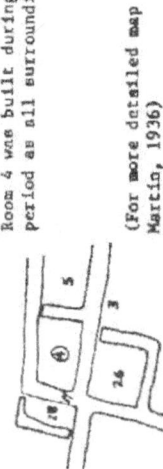

(For more detailed map refer to Paul S. Martin, 1936)

Floor (Floor type: additional notes)
No work was done on floor.

Roof (Roof type: additional notes)
Not ascertainable.

Details (Notes on doorways, lintels, etc.)

Report 20

Condition when work started:
Ancient Masonry:

None of the original masonry remained in this wall.

Repair or reconstruction previous to this work:

Extensive work was done in Room 4 by Al Lancaster in 1966. All walls were capped with two large patches repaired in the east wall. The southwest corner of room was built up and beam seatswere repaired.

Materials, construction, and technique in making repairs or accomplishing job:

Building stones were replaced in areas where they had slipped from wall. Stones were reset with a mixture of Portland Type I and II cement with Shiprock sand. All newly cemented areas were pointed with soil mortar.

Date work started: 8/4/74

Date work finished: 8/5/74

Man days of labor: 4 hrs., 45 minutes

Larry V. Nordby _____8/5/74_____
Archeologist-foreman   Date

a

b

Figure 59. Room 4, southeast interior corner. a, several stones slipped from wall leaving a large gap; b, stones were reset.

RUINS STABILIZATION RECORD

Report ____21____

Room ____13____

Klva _____

RUIN ____Lowry Ruin____

Personnel of party on this job: Wall (interior) _____

KL   (N,E,S,W) North - entrance

                                (Exterior)   x

                    Floor, roof No work done on floor, roof.

References to publications and justifications for job:

Lowry Ruin in Southwestern Colorado: Paul S. Martin, 1936
Field notes of Al Lancaster for 1966-67 stabilization

The east side of north entrance to Rm. 13 was missing several building stones
beneath upper cement cap. The stones had completely eroded out probably due
to water run off and the location of entrance in an area of pueblo which
recieves many visitors.

ARCHITECTURE

Orientation, plan and type (Situation, evidence of additional stories, period
of construction relative to surrounding rooms, evidence of burning, etc.)

Room 13 was built after Rooms 17, 7, 8
and at the same time as room 33.

(For more detailed map refer to Martin,
1936, Fig. 54)

Floor (Floor type: additional notes)

No work was done on floor.

Roof (Roof type: additional notes)

Not ascertainable.

Details (Notes on doorways, lintels, etc.)

East side of north entrance to Room 13.

Report 21

Condition when work started:
Ancient Masonry:

Prehistoric mortar and masonry was eroding out beneath cement cap. Several
stones were missing and mortar was soft and crumbling from wall.

Repair or reconstruction previous to this work:

This entrance was partially rebuilt in 1966-67 by Al Lancaster. Extensive
stabilization was done in other areas of this room. The west end of the
south wall was built up and new lintels were replaced over doorway and one
window. About 14" of wall was built over lintels. All walls were capped and
loose stone was removed from room.

Materials, construction, and technique in making repairs or accomplishing job:

All loose stones were removed and replaced along with those missing from wall.
These stones were reset with a mixture of Portland Type I and II cement and
Shiprock sand. All large joints and newly cemented areas were pointed with a
soil mortar mixture of three parts soil to one part sand.

Date work started: 8/5/74

Date work finished: 8/5/74

Man days of labor: 1 hr., 5 min.

Larry V. Nordby   8/5/74
_____
Archeologist-foreman   Date

Figure 60. Room 13, north exterior entrance. Several stones were reset on the west side of the entrance. No photo was taken before stabilization.

RUINS STABILIZATION RECORD

Report __22__

Room _____

Kiva __H__

RUIN __Lowry Ruin__

Personnel of party on this job: Wall (Interior) __x__

JAL.   (N,E,S,W) __North__

(Exterior) _____

Floor, roof __No work was done on floor, roof.__

References to publications and justifications for job:

Lowry Ruin in Southwestern Colorado; Paul S. Martin, 1936
Field notes of Al Lancaster for 1966-67 stabilization

The north interior wall of Kiva H contained an area where two small building stones had slipped from wall. Replacing these stones stopped further erosion in this area.

ARCHITECTURE

Orientation, plan and type (Situation, evidence of additional stories, period of construction relative to surrounding rooms, evidence of burning, etc.)

Kiva H was built during the same time period as surrounding rooms 30, 29, 2, and 9. Room 26 and 27 were built during the period just previous.

(For more detailed map refer to Paul S. Martin, 1936)

Floor (Floor type: additional notes)

No work was done on floor.

Roof (Roof type: additional notes)

Not ascertainable.

Details (Notes on doorways, lintels, etc.)

Report 22

Condition when work started:
Ancient Masonry:

The north wall of Kiva H has been capped. The area beneath the two course cement cap still contains prehistoric masonry. In most areas of this wall large joints are obvious between building stones where the prehistoric mortar is washing out. There was only one area where stones were missing and this was the area of cement patch.

Repair or reconstruction previous to this work:

The north wall of Kiva H was capped in 1966 by Al Lancaster. Extensive stabilization was done in several areas of Kiva H. A deadman's brace was inserted through north wall from Room 26 with steel plate, to stabilize north wall. The west wall was built up four to five feet also to act as brace for north wall. The ventilator was reconstructed along with firepit. All walls were capped.

Materials, construction, and technique in making repairs or accomplishing job:

Several small building stones were reset in wall with a mixture of Portland Type I and II cement and Shiprock sand.

Date work started: 9/6/74

Date work finished: 9/6/74

Man days of labor: 45 minutes

Larry V. Nordby   9/6/74
Archeologist-foreman   Date

104

Figure 61. Kiva H, north interior wall. A small patch was made with soil mortar where two stones had slipped from the wall. No photo was taken before stabilization.

RUINS STABILIZATION RECORD

Report ___23___

Room _____

Kiva B - pilaster 6

RUIN ___Lowry Ruin___

Personnel of party on this job: Wall (Interior) _____

LKL   (N,E,S,W) _____

                                 (Exterior) _____

                                 Floor, roof _____

References to publications and justifications for job:

Lowry Ruin in Southwestern Colorado; Paul S. Martin, 1936

Field notes of Al Lancaster for 1966-67 stabilization

Pilaster 6 was restored along with the rest of pilasters in Kiva B
along with the partial restoration of Kiva B as a whole.

ARCHITECTURE

Orientation, plan and type (Situation, evidence of additional stories, period
of construction relative to surrounding rooms, evidence of burning, etc.)

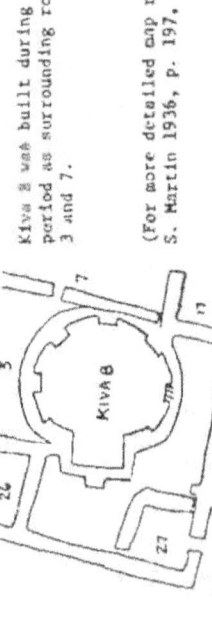

Kiva B was built during the same time
period as surrounding rooms 26, 27,
3 and 7.

(For more detailed map refer to Paul
S. Martin 1936, p. 197, Fig. 53)

Floor (Floor type: additional notes)

No work was done on floor.

Roof (Roof type: additional notes)

Not ascertainable.

Details (Notes on doorways, lintels, etc.)

106

Condition when work started:
Ancient Masonry:

The masonry of pilaster 6 was in poor shape to a depth of 7 courses from top
course. The stones were loose along with mortar.

Repair or reconstruction previous to this work:

No reconstruction was done previous to this time. Kiva B was backfilled
immediately following excavation to protect murals.

Materials, construction, and technique in making repairs or accomplishing job:

All loose stones and soil mortar was removed to a depth of 7 courses then
reset with a mixture of Portland Type I and II with Shiprock sand.

Date work started: 5/29/75

Date work finished: 6/1/75

Man days of labor: 8 hrs., 45 min. = 1 day, 45 min.

Larry V. Nordby   6.1.75
Archeologist-foreman   Date

Report 23

a

b

Figure 62. Kiva B, pilaster 6. a, before stabilization showing the extent of damage; b, after stabilization.

Condition when work started:
Ancient Masonry:

Prehistoric masonry of Pilaster 7 was in good condition aside from the upper 2 feet. These upper courses needed to be reset due to loose stones and crumbling mortar. The masonry of the pilaster consisted of thin slab-laid with thick square blocks.

Repair or reconstruction previous to this work:

No reconstruction was done in Kiva B prior to the 1974 season. Kiva B was excavated in 1936 and backfilled immediately following excavation.

Materials, construction, and technique in making repairs or accomplishing job:

The pilaster was torn down to a stable point where no loose stones or mortar were evident in lower courses. Building stones were reset with a mixture of Rockmont Type I and II cement and Shiprock sand. All cement joints were pointed with a soil mortar mixture of 4 parts soil to 1 part sand.

Date work started: 5/26/75

Date work finished: 5/27/75

Man days of labor: 9 hrs. = 1 day, 1 hr.

Larry V. Nordby   5/27/75
Archeologist-foreman   Date

RUINS STABILIZATION RECORD   Report   24
                                 Room
                                 Kiva B - Pilaster 7

RUIN   Lowry Ruin

Personnel of party on this job: Wall (Interior)   x

                                (N,E,S,W)   East

                                (Exterior)

                LKL, JA

                Floor, roof   No work was done on floor, roof.

References to publications and justifications for job:

Lowry Ruin in Southwestern Colorado; Paul S. Martin, 1936
Field notes of Al Lancaster for 1966-67 stabilization

Pilaster 7 was restored along with other pilasters in Kiva B with the partial restoration of Kiva B.

ARCHITECTURE

Orientation, plan and type (Situation, evidence of additional stories, period
of construction relative to surrounding rooms, evidence of burning, etc.)

Kiva B was built at the same time or
during the same time period as surrounding
rooms 26, 27, 3, and 7.

(For more detailed map refer to Paul
S. Martin 1936, p. 197, Fig. 53)

Floor (Floor type: additional notes)

        No work was done on floor.

Roof (Roof type: additional notes)

        Not ascertainable.

Details (Notes on doorways, lintels, etc.)

a

b

Figure 63.   Kiva B, pilaster 7.   a, before stabilization; b, after
stabilization.

RUIN _____ Lowry Ruin

Personnel of party on this job: Wall (interior) _____ x

CWM, CDB   (N,E,S,W) _____ East

                           (Exterior) _____ x

                Floor, roof _____ No work was done on floor, roof

References to publications and justifications for job:

Lowry Ruin of Southwestern Colorado; Paul S. Martin, 1936
Field notes of Al Lancaster for 1966-67 stabilization

A major justification in restoring the upper courses of the east wall of
Kiva B was to provide a more level base for the permanent roof over Kiva B.

ARCHITECTURE

Orientation, plan and type (Situation, evidence of additional stories, period
of construction relative to surrounding rooms, evidence of burning, etc.)

Kiva was built during the same time
period as surrounding Rooms 26, 27,
3 and 7.

(For more detailed map refer to Paul
S. Martin 1936, p. 197, Fig. 53)

Floor (Floor type: additional notes)

    No work was done on floor.

Roof (Roof type: additional notes)

    No work was done on roof.

Details (Notes on doorways, lintels, etc.)

Condition when work started:
Ancient Masonry:

Prehistoric masonry for the E wall of Kiva B was in good condition
with building stones set firmly in mortar. Mud mortar retained a
hard rough texture. Lack of erosion is probably due to immediate
backfilling in 1936. The masonry for this wall is very rough with
a stone face interior and exterior with rubble fill.

Repair or reconstruction previous to this work:

No restoration was done in the area of Kiva B during 1966-67. In
1974, Kiva B was excavated to 15 cm. above floor surface. At this
time the North portion of this wall was stabilized due to its unsafe
condition (Report 17).

Materials, construction, and technique in making repairs or accomplishing job:

Wall was cleaned off, and in most areas no stone was taken off wall,
but courses were added to top courses. An objective of rebuilding
this wall was to provide a less sloping base for the permanent roof
over Kiva B. In most areas of wall 3-4 courses were added to wall.
Stones were set with a mixture of Portland Type I and II cement and
Shiprock sand.

Date work started: 5/26/75

Date work finished: 6/2/75

Man days of labor: 46 hrs., 45 min. = 5 days, 6 hrs.

                              Larry V. Nordby   6/2/75
                        _____
                        Archeologist-foreman   Date

Condition when work started:

Ancient Masonry:

This wall was capped in 1966 and no ancient masonry remained in areas involving this job.

Repair or reconstruction previous to this work:

The east wall of Rm. 29 was stabilized and reconstructed in 1966 by Al Lancaster. The entire wall was built up four to five feet to a base plate which extended through wall into Room 27 and formed a deadman's brace.

Materials, construction, and technique in making repairs or accomplishing job:

Old stone was reused with a mixture of Portland Type I and II cement and Shiprock sand. Joints were pointed and grouted with soil cement of 2 parts soil to 1 part cement.

Date work started: 5/30/75

Date work finished: 6/1/75

Man days of labor: 30 hours, 40 min. - 3 days, 1 hour, 20 min.

Larry V. Nordby _____ 6/1/75 _____
Archeologist-foreman _____ Date

RUINS STABILIZATION RECORD

Report _____ 26 _____

Room _____ 29 _____

Kiva _____

RUIN _____ Lowry Ruin _____

Personnel of party on this job: Wall (Interior) _____ x _____

ASW, JA _____ (N,E,S,W) _____ East _____

(Exterior) _____

Floor, roof _____ No work was done on floor, roof.

References to publications and justifications for job:

Lowry Ruin in Southwestern Colorado; Paul Martin, 1936
Field notes of Al Lancaster for 1966-67 stabilization

A permanent roof was built over Kiva B in 1973. With the additional weight of this roof on the areas surrounding Kiva B it was necessary to step up the W wall of Kiva H to add support to the N wall.

ARCHITECTURE

Orientation, plan and type (Situation, evidence of additional stories, period of construction relative to surrounding rooms, evidence of burning, etc.)

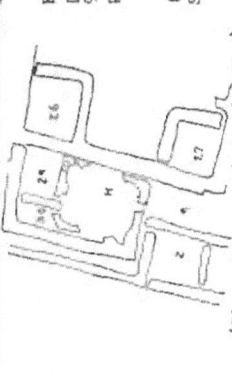

Kiva H was built during the same time period as surrounding rooms 30, 29, 2, and 9. Rooms 26 and 27 were built during the period just previous.

(For a more detailed map refer to Paul S. Martin, 1936)

Floor (Floor type: additional notes)

No work was done on floor.

Roof (Roof type: additional notes)

No work was done on roof.

Details (Notes on doorways, lintels, etc.)

111

a

b

Figure 64.   Room 29, east interior wall. a, view of wall before it
was stepped up to brace the north wall; b, wall after courses were
added.

RUINS STABILIZATION RECORD

Report ___ 27

Room ___

Kiva ___ B-Pilaster 5

RUIN ___ Lowry Ruin

Personnel of party on this job: Wall (Interior) ___

(N,E,S,W) ___

(Exterior) ___

Floor, roof ___ No work done.

LkL

References to publications and justifications for job:

Lowry Ruin in Southwestern Colorado; Paul S. Martin, 1936
Field notes of Al Lancaster for 1966-67 stabilization

The upper portion of pilaster 5 had loose stones and mud mortar with stones
missing in several areas. The pilaster needed to be rebuilt aprox. 66 cm. to
reach it's original height. Pilaster 5 was restored along with the rest of pilasters
in Kiva B.

ARCHITECTURE

Orientation, plan and type (Situation, evidence of additional stories, period
of construction relative to surrounding rooms, evidence of burning, etc.)

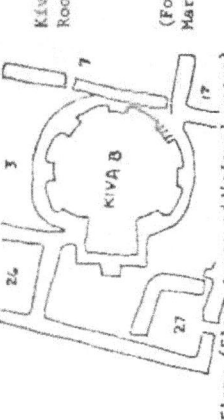

Kiva B was built at the same time as surrounding
Rooms 26, 27, 3, and 7.

(For more detailed map refer to Paul S.
Martin, 1936, p. 197, Fig. 53)

Floor (Floor type: additional notes)

No work done.

Roof (Roof type: additional notes)

No work done.

Details (Notes on doorways, lintels, etc.)

No work done.

Condition when work started:
Ancient Masonry:

The ancient masonry was in good condition in all areas except for the upper
courses where the soil mortar was falling out and stones were loose and missing.

Repair or reconstruction previous to this work:

No repair or reconstruction was done previously, this area was backfilled
after excavation in 1936, to protect murals.

Materials, construction, and technique in making repairs or accomplishing job:

Old stone was relaid to 66cm. to original height with a cement mixture of
Portland Type I and II cement and Shiprock sand with 9 oz. of light Buff
coloring added. Joints were pointed to a depth of ½" and pointed with a
soil mortar of 4 parts soil to 1 part sand.

Date work started: 5/30/75

Date work finished: 6/4/75

Man days of labor: 8 hrs. = 1 day

Larry V. Nordby ___ 6/4/75

Archeologist-foreman ___ Date

113

a

b

Figure 65. Kiva B, pilaster 5. a, pilaster before stabilization; b,
about 66cm. was added to pilaster, also new shelves to either side of
pilaster 5.

RUINS STABILIZATION RECORD

Report _____ 28 _____

Room _____

Kiva B-Pilaster 4

RUIN _____ Lowry Ruin _____

Personnel of party on this job: Wall (Interior) _____

ECA, LKL   (N,E,S,W) _____

                  (Exterior) _____

                  Floor, roof _____

References to publications and justifications for job:

Lowry Ruin in Southwestern Colorado; Paul S. Martin, 1936
Field Notes of Al Lancaster for 1966-67 Stabilization

Pilaster 4 was reconstructed along with other pilasters in Kiva B.

ARCHITECTURE

Orientation, plan and type (Situation, evidence of additional stories, period
of construction relative to surrounding rooms, evidence of burning, etc.)

Kiva B was built at the same time as surrounding
rooms 26, 27, 3 and 7.

(For more detailed map refer to Paul
S. Martin, 1936, p. 197, Fig. 53)

Floor (Floor type: additional notes)

No work was done on floor.

Roof (Roof type: additional notes)

Not ascertainable.

Details (Notes on doorways, lintels, etc.)

No work was done on doorway, lintels, etc.

115

Report 28

Condition when work started:
Ancient Masonry:

The ancient masonry of Pilaster 4 was in poor shape from 48-68 cm. below
original height. Building stones in this area were loose in some places and
missing in others. The soil mortar was crumbling and soft.

Repair or reconstruction previous to this work:

No reconstruction was previously done in Kiva B since it was backfilled immediately following excavation to preserve murals.

Materials, construction, and technique in making repairs or accomplishing job:

Pilaster was reconstructed with reused stone from 48-88 cm. in height to
original height. A cement mixture of Portland Type I and II cement and
Shiprock sand. Joints were grouted to a depth of ½ inch and pointed with a
soil mortar mixture of 4 parts soil to 1 part sand.

Date work started: 6/2/75

Date work finished: 6/4/75

Man days of labor: 12 hours = 1 day, 4 hours.

_____ Larry V. Nordby _____   6/4/75 _____
Archeologist-foreman   Date

Figure 66. Kiva B, pilaster 4. Pilaster was stepped into the west wall of Kiva A. No photo was taken before stabilization.

RUINS STABILIZATION RECORD   Report _____ 29

Report 29

RUIN   Lowry Ruin   Room _____

                                      Kiva B- Southern Recess

Personnel of party on this job: Wall (interior) ___x___

        CWM   (N,E,S,W) ___South___

                                (Exterior) _____

                    Floor, roof No work was done on floor, roof.

References to publications and justifications for job:

Lowry Ruin in Southwestern Colorado; Paul S. Martin, 1936
Field notes of Al Lancaster for 1966-67 Stabilization

Before reconstruction the southern recess was structurally unstable with
building stones and mortar falling from the upper courses. The restoration
of the southern recess was a part of the restoration of Kiva B as a whole.

ARCHITECTURE

Orientation, plan and type (Situation, evidence of additional stories, period
of construction relative to surrounding rooms, evidence of burning, etc.)

        Kiva B was built during the same time
        period as surrounding Rooms 26, 27, 3 and 7.

        (For a more detailed map refer to Paul S.
        Martin 1936, p. 197, Fig. 53)

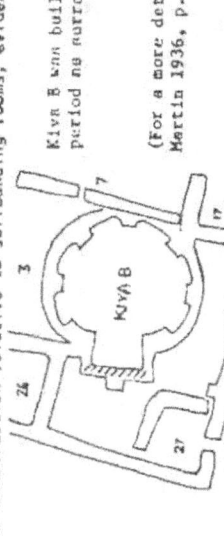

Floor (Floor type: additional notes)

        No work done.

Roof (Roof type: additional notes)

        Not ascertainable.

Details (Notes on doorways, lintels, etc.)

Condition when work started:
Ancient Masonry:

Entire area to be restored contained prehistoric masonry. Building stones
were loose and falling from upper courses to a depth of 57 cm. at the greatest
point. Soil mortar was soft and crumbling from wall.

Repair or reconstruction previous to this work:

No reconstruction had previously been done in Kiva B which was backfilled
following excavation in 1936 to protect murals.

Materials, construction, and technique in making repairs or accomplishing job:

Old stone was reused to reset upper courses of the southern recess. These
stones were reset with a mixture of Portland Type I and II cement and Shiprock
sand, joints were grouted to a depth of ¼ inch and a soil mortar of 4 parts
soil to 1 part sand was pointed into joints.

Date work started: 5/28/75

Date work finished: 6/3/75

Man days of labor: 37 hours = 4 days, 5 hours

                              Larry V. Nordby   6/3/75

                              Archeologist-foreman   Date

RUINS STABILIZATION RECORD Report ___30___

Room _____

Kiva B- Pilaster 3

RUIN _____Lowry Ruin_____

Personnel of party on this job: Wall (interior)_____

(N,E,S,W)_____

ECA

(Exterior)_____

Floor, roof No work done on floor, roof.

References to publications and justifications for job:

Lowry Ruin in Southwestern Colorado; Paul S. Martin 1936
Field notes of Al Lancaster for 1966-67 Stabilization

Pilaster 3 was reconstructed along with the other pilasters in Kiva B as a
part of the restoration of Kiva B.

ARCHITECTURE

Orientation, plan and type (Situation, evidence of additional stories, period
of construction relative to surrounding rooms, evidence of burning, etc.)

Kiva B was built during the same time
period as surrounding Rooms 26,27, 3
and 7.

(For more detailed map refer to Paul S.
Martin p. 197, Fig. 53)

Floor (Floor type: additional notes)

No work was done on floor.

Roof (Roof type: additional notes)

Not ascertainable.

Details (Notes on doorways, lintels, etc.)

118

Report 30

Condition when work started:
Ancient Masonry:

Much of the original pilaster was still in good shape retaining it's original
shape. The area showing the most erosion was the front veneer of the pilaster,
the damage did not extend through the thickness of pilaster. The upper 2
courses had to be reset the thickness of pilaster and the front veneer to a
depth of 85 cm.

Repair or reconstruction previous to this work:

No reconstruction had previously been done in Kiva B which was backfilled
following excavation in 1936 to protect murals.

Materials, construction, and technique in making repairs or accomplishing job:

Old stone was reset with a mixture of Portland Type I and II cement. All
joints were grouted ½ inch and pointed with a soil mortar mixture of 4
parts soil to 1 part sand.

Date work started: 6/4/75

Date work finished: 6/5/75

Man days of labor: 7 hours.

_____Larry V. Nordby_____   6/5/75

Archeologist-foreman   Date

a

b

Figure 67. Kiva B, pilaster 3. a, before stabilization; b, after
stabilization and painting of the joints.

RUINS STABILIZATION RECORD

Report __31__

Room __Kiva B- Pilaster 1__

RUIN __Lowry Ruin__

Personnel of party on this Job: Wall (Interior) _____

CWM (N,E,S,W) _____

(Exterior) _____

Floor, roof __No work was done on floor, roof.__

References to publications and justifications for Job:

Lowry Ruin in Southwestern Colorado; Paul S. Martin 1936
Field notes of Al Lancaster for 1966-67 Stabilization

Pilaster 1 was restored along with other pilasters in Kiva B as part of the restoration of Kiva B.

ARCHITECTURE

Orientation, plan and type (situation, evidence of additional stories, period of construction relative to surrounding rooms, evidence of burning, etc.)

Kiva B was built during the same time period as surrounding Rooms 26, 27, 3 and 7.

(For more detailed map refer to Paul S. Martin, p. 197, Fig. 53)

Floor (Floor type: additional notes)

No work was done.

Roof (Roof type: additional notes)

No work was done on roof.

Details (Notes on doorways, lintels, etc.)

Condition when work started:
Ancient Masonry:

A large portion of the upper courses of Pilaster 1 were missing or partially eroded. Pilaster 1 needed to be rebuilt the entire thickness of pilaster from 40-86 cm. in height.

Repair or reconstruction previous to this work:

No reconstruction was done previously in Kiva B. Kiva B was backfilled following excavation in 1936 to protect murals.

Materials, construction, and technique in making repairs or accomplishing Job:

Old stone was reused with a mixture of Portland Type I and II cement and Shiprock sand. All joints were grouted to a depth of ½ inch then pointed with a soil mortar mixture of 4 parts soil to 1 part cement.

Date work started: 6/4/75

Date work finished: 6/6/75

Man days of labor: 15 hours = 1 day, 7 hrs.
(grouting time excluded, refer to Report 45)

Larry V. Nordby _____ 6/6/75

Archeologist-foreman   Date

a

b

Figure 68. Kiva B, pilaster 1. a, before stabilization; b, after
stabilization.

RUINS STABILIZATION RECORD

Report 32
Room
Kiva B-Pilaster 2

RUIN   Lowry Ruin

Personnel of party on this job: Wall (Interior)

        (N,E,S,W)

        JH, ECA

        (Exterior) No work was done on floor, roof.

        Floor, roof

References to publications and justifications for job:

Lowry Ruin in Southwestern Colorado; Paul S. Martin 1936
Field notes of Al Lancaster for 1966-67 Stabilization

Pilaster was restored along with the other pilasters in Kiva B as part of the
complete restoration of Kiva B.

ARCHITECTURE

Orientation, plan and type (situation, evidence of additional stories, period
of construction relative to surrounding rooms, evidence of burning, etc.)

Kiva B was built during the same time
period as surrounding rooms 26, 27, 3
and 7.

(For a more detailed map refer to Paul
S. Martin 1936, p. 197, Fig. 53)

Floor (Floor type: additional notes)

        No work was done on floor.

Roof (Roof type: additional notes)

        No work was done on roof.

Details (Notes on doorways, lintels, etc.)

Condition when work started:
Ancient Masonry:

The prehistoric masonry of pilaster 2 was in very poor condition through the
entire thickness of the pilaster. Building stones to a depth of 100-105 cm.
needed to be removed from top of pilaster and reset.

Repair or reconstruction previous to this work:

No reconstruction was done previous to this time. Kiva B was backfilled
following excavation to preserve murals.

Materials, construction, and technique in making repairs or accomplishing job:

Pilaster 2 was taken down to a depth of 100-105 cm. and all loose stone and mortar
were removed. Building stones were reset with a mixture of 3 parts Portland
cement Type I and II and Shiprock sand. A new peg aprox. 1 inch in diameter
by 11 cm. in length was set in the front of pilaster in socket left by
prehistoric peg.

Date work started: 6/4/75

Date work finished: 6/6/75

Man days of labor: 22 hours, 30 min. - 2 days, 6 hrs, 30 min.

                                        Larry V. Nordby   6/6/75
                                        Archeologist-Foreman   Date

Figure 69. Kiva B, pilaster 2. View after stabilization. No
photo was taken before stabilization.

Condition when work started:
Ancient Masonry:

In most areas where soil mortar was applied no prehistoric masonry remained since soil mortar was applied over cement joints. Two areas were worked which were an exception. Pilaster 6 had an area on the lower portion which was a gaping hole resulting from missing stone. This hole was filled with soil mortar and smoothed to resemble surrounding plaster. A small area of floor was repaired over the ventilation shaft.

Repair or reconstruction previous to this work:

No repair or reconstruction was done previous to the 1974-75 field season. Kiva B was backfilled immediately following excavation to preserve murals.

Materials, construction, and technique in making repairs or accomplishing job:

A soil mortar of 4 parts soil to 1 part sand was used on the walls of Kiva B. The mortar was kneaded to a stiff consistency before being pressed between cement joints.
A wetter mortar was used in the reconstruction of a portion of the floor surface. This mortar was applied to a wet scraped surface then continually smoothed with a trowel until smooth and hard. This takes constant attention, since cracking occurs as mortar dries.

Date work started: 6/10/75

Date work finished: 6/13/75

Men days of labor: 29 hours, 25 min. = 3 days, 5 hrs., 25 min.

Larry V. Nordby   6/13/75

Archaeologist-foreman   Date

RUINS STABILIZATION RECORD

Report _____ 33 _____

Room _____

Kiva _____ B _____

RUIN _____ Lowry Ruin _____

Personnel of party on this job: Wall (Interior) ___x___

(N,E,S,W) _N, E, S, and W._

(Exterior) _____

Floor, roof _____

References to publications and justifications for job:

Lowry Ruin in Southwestern Colorado; Paul S. Martin, 1936
Field notes of Al Lancaster for 1965-67 Stabilization

Pointing all newly cemented joints was done as part of the restoration of Kiva B. Pointing with soil mortar blends the prehistoric areas with the newly reconstructed areas.

ARCHITECTURE

Orientation, plan and type (Situation, evidence of additional stories, period of construction relative to surrounding rooms, evidence of burning, etc.)

Kiva B was built during the same building period as surrounding Rooms 26, 27, 3 and 7.

(For more detailed map refer to Paul S. Martin, p. 197, Fig. 53)

Floor (Floor type: additional notes)

A portion of the floor above the underground ventilation shaft was destroyed when vent shaft was reroofed to 1936. This area was reconstructed by spreading a soil mortar over it and smoothing it out to make a new floor.

Roof (Roof type: additional notes)

Not ascertainable.

Details (Notes on doorways, lintels, etc.)

The entranceway into Kiva B through the southern recess was pointed with soil mortar over newly laid cement joints.

124

Figure 70. Kiva B, interior walls. Floor near the gate has been resurfaced and all newly cemented joints have been covered with soil mortar.

Condition when work started:
Ancient Masonry:

The masonry of E doorway of Rm. 27 was in good condition. The lower portion of T-shaped doorway below the bench was what was stabilized. This area only was a few loose stones with stones entirely missing from the step.

Repair or reconstruction previous to this work:

The East wall of Rm. 27 was reconstructed in 1966 by Al Lancaster and crew. In 1966 the wall was in very poor condition and a primary portion of it had to be rebuilt. The doorway was plugged prehistorically. This plug was removed and doorway was reconstructed with new lintels. The ground surface of Room 31 was raised to just above the bench of doorway. Only the portion of doorway above bench was restored.

Materials, construction, and technique in making repairs or accomplishing job:

All loose stones surrounding entrance way were removed and reset along with stones for step. These stones were reset with a mixture of Portland Type I and II cement with Shiprock sand. A soil mortar of 4 parts soil to 1 part cement was pointed over cement joints.

Date work started: 6/10/75

Date work finished: 6/12/75

Man days of labor: 22 hours = 2 days, 6 hours

Larry V. Nordby   6/12/75
Archeologist-foreman   Date

RUINS STABILIZATION RECORD   Report _____ 34 _____

Room _____ 27 _____

Kiva _____

RUIN _____ Lowry Ruin _____

Personnel of party on this job: Wall (Interior) _____ x _____

(N, E, S, W) _____ East _____

(Exterior) _____ x _____

ECA

Floor, roof _____ No work was done on floor, roof. _____

References to publications and justifications for job:

Lowry Ruin in Southwestern Colorado; Paul S. Martin, 1936
Field notes of Al Lancaster for 1966-67 Stabilization

The lower portion of the east doorway of Rm. 27 was excavated and stabilized to provide counter excess in Kiva B. The previous only partially excavated doorway provided a very low entrance.

ARCHITECTURE

Orientation, plan and type (Situation, evidence of additional stories, period of construction relative to surrounding rooms, evidence of burning, etc.)

Room 27 was built during the same time period as Kiva B. Other surrounding rooms 9, 31, 32, and Kiva H were built during a later period.

(For a more detailed map refer to Martin 1936, p. 197, Fig. 53)

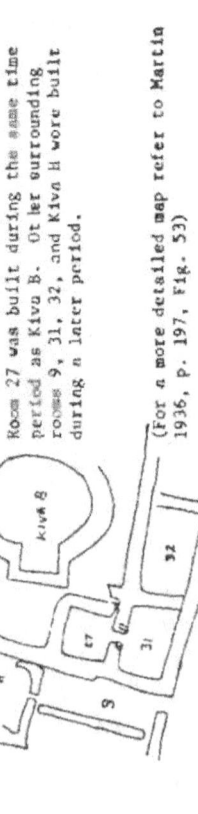

Floor (Floor type: additional notes)

No work was done on floor.

Roof (Roof type: additional notes)

Not ascertainable.

Details (Notes on doorways, lintels, etc.)

Lintels of doorway were replaced in 1966 by Al Lancaster and crew. This report primarily covers the replacement of step.

a

b

Figure 71. Room 27, east exterior entrance. a, entrance before
stabilization in 1965; b, after stabilization in 1965 room was
filled to above "T" of doorway.

c

Figure 71. Room 27, east exterior entrance. c, after excavation and stabilization.

Condition when work started:
Ancient Masonry:

Only a small portion of the original wall remained of Kiva A. The rest was probably torn down with the excavation of Kiva B.

Repair or reconstruction previous to this work:

No reconstruction was done previous to this time. Kiva A and B were backfilled immediately following excavation.

Materials, construction, and technique in making repairs or accomplishing job:

A single wall was reconstructed on the base of the original wall of Kiva A. Old stone was reused with a mixture of Portland Type I and II cement and Shiprock sand. This wall was pointed with a thin slap of soil mortar.

Date work started: 5/29/75
Date work finished: 6/3/75
Man days of labor: 77 hrs. 15 min. = 9 days, 5 hours, 15 min.

Larry V. Nordby _____ 6/3/75 _____
Archeologist-foreman   Date

RUINS STABILIZATION RECORD

Report ___35___
Room _____
Kiva ___A___

RUIN Lowry Ruin

Personnel of party on this job: Wall (Interior) ____x____

    ECA, JAH   (N,E,S,W) ___west-northwest___

        (Exterior) _____

    Floor, roof No work was done on floor, roof.

References to publications and justifications for job:

Lowry Ruin in Southwestern Colorado; Paul S. Martin, 1936
Field notes of Al Lancaster for 1966-67 Stabilization

The southwest interior wall of Kiva A was rebuilt primarily as a retaining wall to keep loose dirt out of Kiva A. Wall was also rebuilt to provide a foundation for base plate of roof.

ARCHITECTURE

Orientation, plan and type (Situation, evidence of additional stories, period of construction relative to surrounding rooms, evidence of burning, etc.)

Rooms 26, 3, 7, 27, and 17 surrounding Kiva A were all built in the period previous to the one Kiva A was built in.

(For more detailed map refer to Martin 1936, p. 197-199, Fig. 53 and 54)

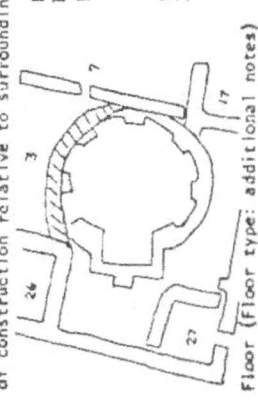

Floor (Floor type: additional notes)

None of floor remains.

Roof (Roof type: additional notes)

Not ascertainable.

Details (Notes on doorways, lintels, etc.)

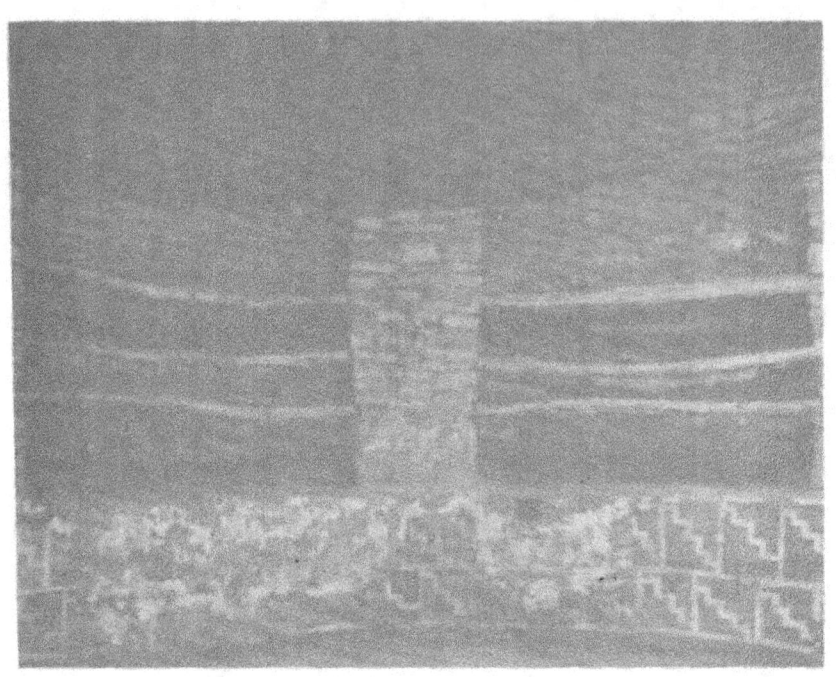

Figure 72. Kiva A, west wall. West view of wall after stabilization as retaining wall and as a foundation for roof.

RUINS STABILIZATION RECORD

Report ___36___
Room ___31___
Kiva _____

RUIN ___Lowry Ruin___

Personnel of party on this job: Wall (interior)   x

    LVH, ASW, JA   (N,E,S,W) ___North___

                 (Exterior)

           Floor, roof No work was done on floor or roof.

References to publications and justifications for job:

Lowry Ruin in Southwestern Colorado: Paul S. Martin, 1936
Field notes of Al Lancaster for 1966-67 stabilization.

This wall was built up to act as a brace for the west wall.

ARCHITECTURE

Orientation, plan and type (Situation, evidence of additional stories, period
of construction relative to surrounding rooms, evidence of burning, etc.)

Rm. 31 was built during the last building
phase of Lowry. Surrounding rms. 9, 32, 37,
and 36 were built during the same time
period. Kiva A and rm. 27 were built
earlier.

(For a more detailed map refer to Paul
S. Martin 1936, p. 197-198, Fig. 53)

Floor (Floor type: additional notes)

    No work was done on the floor.

Roof (Roof type: additional notes)

    Not ascertainable.

Details (Notes on doorways, lintels, etc.)

131

Report 36

Condition when work started:
Ancient Masonry:

No prehistoric masonry remained.

Repair or reconstruction previous to this work:

Al Lancaster raised this wall as a brace in 1966-67 also.

Materials, construction, and technique in making repairs or accomplishing job:

Wall was stepped up about 5 courses to brace the west wall. Old stone was
reused with a mixture of Portland Type I and II cement and Shiprock sand.
Area was pointed with soil cement.

Date work started: 5/29/75
Date work finished: 6/27/75
Man days of labor: 14 hours = 1 day 5 hours

_____   _____
Archeologist-foreman   Date

a

b

Figure 73. Room 31, north interior wall. a, before wall was stepped up as a brace to the west wall; b, after stabilization.

REFERENCES CITED

Breternitz, David A.
   1975   Mesa Verde Research Center, 1975. Southwestern Lore 41:3:17-21.

DiPeso, Charles C.
   1974   Casas Grandes, A Fallen Trading Center of the Gran Chichimeca,
             Volume 1. Northland Press, Flagstaff.

Eddy, Frank W.
   1972   Archaeological Report Covering the Chimney Rock Site Survey
             and Excavations at the Chimney Rock Pueblo, 5AA83. Sub-
             mitted to the U.S. Forest Service, San Juan National Forest,
             Durango.

Lancaster, James A.
   1967   Unpublished field notes for 1966-67 restoration of Lowry
             Ruin.

Martin, Paul S.
   1936   Lowry Ruin in Southwestern Colorado. Anthropological Series,
             Field Museum of Natural History, Vol. 23, No. 1.

   1974   "Lowry Ruin and the Anasazi Culture,"   Archaeological
             Research in Retrospect", edited by C.W. Willey and J.
             Sabloff, pp. 8-12. Winthrop Pubs. Inc., Cambridge.

Robinson, W. J. and Bruce G. Harrill
   1974   Tree-Ring Dates from Colorado V: Mesa Verde Area. Laboratory
             of Tree-Ring Research, University of Arizona, Tucson.

APPENDIX A

Correlation of Archaeological Features and

Stabilization Reports

Room No.	Report No.		Page
4	20	....	100-101
8	11	....	78-75
10	13	....	83-85
11	5	....	61-62
	13	....	83-85
12	1	....	51-52
	9	....	74-75
13	21	....	102-103
14	2	....	53-54
	8	....	72-73
16	7	....	69-71
18	2	....	53-54
21	4	....	58-60
	19	....	97-99
23	15	....	88-90
24	18	....	95-96
27	14	....	86-87
	34	....	126-128
29	26	....	111-112
31	10	....	76-77
	36	....	131-132

Room No.	Report No.		Page
33	12	....	88-82
Kiva A	35	....	129-130
Kiva B	17	....	93-94
	23-25	....	106-110
	27-33	....	113-124
Space E. of Kiva B	16	....	91-92
Kiva E	3	....	55-57
Kiva H	22	....	104-105
Great Kiva	6	....	63-68

APPENDIX B

Tabulation of Labor and Materials, Stabilization

Reports

REPORT	1	2a	2b	3a	3b	4
TECHNIQUE	-cement patch -soil mortar	-cement patch -soil mortar	-cement patch	-cement patch -soil mortar	-cement patch -soil mortar	-cement patch -soil mortar
AREA	7 courses in width x 1m in length	5 courses in width x 1m 30cm in length	2 stones reset	5 courses in width x 1m 50cm	2 stones reset	6 courses in width x 2m in length
# WORKERS	2	2	1	2	1	2
CEMENT						
SAND	6	15	4	15	3	27
CEMENT	2	5	1 1/3	5	1	9
TIME	2 hr.	3 hr.	1 hr.	3 hr. 15 min.	15 min.	9 hr.
# WORKERS	2	2		2	1	1
SOIL MORTAR						
SOIL	2	2		2	2	3
SAND	1	1		1	1	1
TIME	45 min	45 min		45 min	45 min	6 hr.
# WORKERS						
MISC.						
MATERIALS						
TIME						
TOTAL TIME	5 hr. 30 min.	7 hr. 30 min	1 hr.	8 hr.	1 hr.	24 hr.

137

REPORT	5	6	7	8	9	10
TECHNIQUE	-cement patch / -soil mortar	-soil mortar patches	-Rebar / -Cement patch / -soil mortar	-cement patch / -soil mortar	-cement patches / -soil mortar	-cement patch / -soil mortar
AREA	6 courses x 1m 40cm	4 patches of several stones	1.5 x 1.8m	2 stones reset	Several stones reset large joints grouted	4-5 courses in width x 1m in length
# WORKERS	1		2	1	1	1
CEMENT — SAND	12		99	9	6	32
CEMENT — CEMENT	4		33	3	2	12
TIME	7 hr. 30 min		4½ hr.	3 hr.	4 hr. 35 min	12 hr.
# WORKERS	1	1	3	1	1	1
SOIL MORTAR — SOIL	3	2	3	3	2	3
SOIL MORTAR — SAND	1	1	1	1	1	1
TIME	11 hr.	6 hr.	24 hr.	1 hr.	3 hr.	3 hr.
# WORKERS			2			
MISC.			rebar support			
MATERIALS			board braces rebar			
TIME			4 hr.			
TOTAL TIME	18 hr. 30 min	6 hr.	168 hr.	4 hr.	12 hr. 35 min	15 hr.

REPORT	11a	11b	12	13a	13b	13c
TECHNIQUE	-soil mortar	-cement patch -soil mortar	-soil mortar	-cement patches -soil mortar	-cement patch -soil mortar	-cement patch -soil mortar
AREA	All areas where mortar had crumbled	Lintel and other loose stones reset	All large joints	6 stones reset	1 course of several stones	2 stones reset
# WORKERS		1		1	1	1
CEMENT SAND		12		4½	9	9
CEMENT CEMENT		4		1½	3	3
TIME		3 hr.		1 hr.	2 hr.	2 hr.
# WORKERS	2	1	3	1	1	1
SOIL MORTAR SOIL	2	3	2	2	2	3
SOIL MORTAR SAND	1	1	1	1	1	1
TIME	2 hr.	45 min	4 hr.	45 min.	10 min	15 min
# WORKERS						
MISC						
MATERIALS						
TIME						
TOTAL TIME	4 hr.	3 hr. 45 min.	12 hr.	1 hr. 45 min.	2 hr. 10 min.	2 hr. 15 min.

REPORT	14	15	16	17	18	19
TECHNIQUE	-cement patch	-cement patch	-cement patch	-cement patch and cap	-cement patch -soil mortar	-cement patch
AREA	3-4 courses in width x 75cm	5-6 courses in width x 1.3m in length	6 courses in width x 2m in length	6 courses in width x 2m in length - complete thickness of wall	2 courses in width x 3.75m in length	Several stones reset on either side of doorway
# WORKERS	1	1	1	2	2	1
CEMENT SAND	18	21	30	60	33	30
CEMENT	6	7	10	20	11	10
TIME	16 hr.	5 hr. 15 min.	6 hr.	16 hr.	5 hr.	8 hr.
# WORKERS		1		2	2	1
SOIL MORTAR SOIL		3		4	2	3
SAND		1		1	1	1
TIME		1 hr.		2 hr.	4 hr.	1 hr. 20 min.
# WORKERS						
MISC.						
MATERIALS						
TIME						
TOTAL TIME	16 hr.	6 hr. 15 min.	6 hr.	36 hr.	18 hr.	9 hr. 20 min.

REPORT	20	21	22	23	24	25
TECHNIQUE	-cement patch	-cement patch -soil mortar	-cement patch	-cement -soil mortar	-cement -soil mortar	-cement cap
AREA	4 stones reset and large joints grouted	5 stones reset	2 stones reset	Rebuilt to original height	Rebuilt to ori-ginal height	3-4 courses in width x 4m in length
# WORKERS	1	1	1	1	1	1
CEMENT						
SAND	12	6	3	22	16	97
CEMENT	4	2	1	7 1/3	5 1/3	33 1/3
TIME	4 hr.	45 min	45 min	8 hr. 45 min.	9 hr.	46 hr. 45 min
# WORKERS	1	1				
SOIL MORTAR						
SOIL	3	3		(Report 33)	(Report 33)	
SAND	1	1				
TIME	45 min.	20 min.				
# WORKERS				1		
MISC				-peg replaced -rebar support		
MATERIALS				9"x1" peg; 1½" gal nail 2-24' sec. rebar		
TIME				(Included in cement work)		
TOTAL TIME	4 hr. 45 min.	1 hr. 5 min.	45 min.	8 hr. 45 min.	9 hr.	46 hr. 45 min

141

REPORT	26	27	28	29	30	31
TECHNIQUE	-cement cap -soil cement	-cement -soil mortar	-cement -soil mortar	-cement patch -soil mortar	-cement -soil mortar	-cement -soil mortar
AREA	4-5 courses added as brace to N. Wall	Rebuilt to original height	Rebuilt to original height	All upper courses to a depth of 5-6 courses	Rebuilt to original height	Rebuilt to original height
# WORKERS	2	1	1	1	1	1
CEMENT SAND	21	27	25	86	8	34
CEMENT	7	9	8 1/3	28 2/3	2 2/3	11 1/3
TIME	13 hr. 20 min	8 hr.	12 hr.	37 hr.	7 hr.	15 hr.
# WORKERS						
SOIL MORTAR SOIL		(Report 33)	(Report 33)	(Report 33)	(Report 33)	(Report 33)
SAND						
TIME						
# WORKERS	1	1	1		1	
MISC.	soil cement	Peg replaced Rebar support	Peg replaced		Peg replaced	
MATERIALS	2 - Sand 1 - Cement	8"x1" peg 2-2½' sec. of rebar	7" x 1" peg		5½" x 1" peg	
TIME	4 hr.	(included in cement work)	(included in cement work)		(included in cement work)	
TOTAL TIME	30 hr. 40 min	8 hr.	12 hr.	37 hr.	7 hr.	15 hr.

REPORT	32	33	34	35	36
TECHNIQUE	-cement -soil mortar	-soil mortar	-cement patches	-cement	-cement cap -soil cement
AREA	Rebuilt to original height	All cemented areas covered with mortar	Several stones reset in doorway	Most of wall was rebuilt	Wall built up 5-6 courses as brace
# WORKERS	1	1	1	2	2
CEMENT					
SAND	34		16	92	39
CEMENT	11 1/3		5 1/2	28 2/3	13
TIME	22 hr. 30 min		13 hr.	38 hr. 30 min	6 hr. 30 min
# WORKERS		1-3	3		
SOIL MORTAR					
SOIL	(Report 33)	4	3		
SAND		1	1		
TIME		29 hr. 25 min	3 hr.		
# WORKERS	1			1	1
MISC.	Peg replaced			soil paint applied to joints	soil cement
MATERIALS	4'x1" peg			-soil paint	6 - Sand 2 - Cement
TIME	(included in cement work)			15 min.	1 hr.
TOTAL TIME	22 hr. 30 min.	29 hr. 25 min.	22 hr	77 hr. 15 min.	14 hr

APPENDIX C

Tabulation of Labor and Materials, by area

AREA	KIVA B	WHEEL BARREL RAMP	KIVA A W. WALL	KIVA B	KIVA B
TYPE OF JOB	Excavation to 15-20cm above floor	Construction of ramp	Temporary retaining wall	Draping murals with plastic sheeting	Building of temporary roof
# WORKERS			2		
CEMENT / SAND / CEMENT			No information was kept, wall was torn down in 1975.		
TIME			1 hr.		
# WORKERS	3-7	2		3	1-3
MISC. WORK	Excavation	construction of ramp		Draping plastic from tops of walls to above floor	Completely sealing Kiva B
MATERIALS		Amount & size of lumber: 6 - 1x6x12, 1 - 2x4x10, 3 - 2x6x10, 4 - 2x8x14, 4 - 2x12x14, 16 penny nails		1 roll poly. (004) plastic sheeting (6m 10x100) 300 sq. ft.	Refer to description
TIME	348 hr.	1 hr.		3 hr.	62 hr.
TOTAL TIME	348 hr.	2 hr.	2 hr.	9 hr.	62 hr.

AREA	Room 27 N. Int. Wall	KIVA B	KIVA B	KIVA B	KIVA B	KIVA B
TYPE OF JOB	Enlarging of small hole as drainage for roof	Removal of temporary roof	Tracing and photographing murals	Hole made in E. side of S. recess as doorway	Stone steps built into access through E. side of S. recess	Both sides of access entryway veneered
# WORKERS					2	2
CEMENT						
SAND					14	129
CEMENT					4 2/3	43
TIME					3 hr.	41 hr.
# WORKERS	1	6	2	1		2
MISC. WORK	Several stones were removed from wall	Complete removal of roof	Tracing murals arts plastic with photographs to match	Taking stones out of wall to create doorway		Soil mortar to cover cement joints
MATERIALS	none	none	Plastic sheeting, film, felt tip pen	none		Soil mortar proportions 4 - soil/ 1 - sand
TIME	45 min	3 hr.	4 hr.	3 hr.		6 hr.
TOTAL TIME	45 min	18 hr.	8 hr.	3 hr.	3 hr.	34 hr.

AREA	KIVA A	ROOMS 27 & 30	ROOM 27 N. INT. WALL	SPACE BETWEEN ROOM 27 & KIVA B	SPACE E. OF KIVA B
	Retaining wall built on the S. recess of Kiva A	Excavation	Drain hole was enlarged to build doorway	Curtain wall built to connect two areas	Retaining wall built to keep fill out of entry
# WORKERS	1		1	1	1
CEMENT					
SAND	75		68	9	72
CEMENT	25		32 2/3	3	24
TIME	27 hr. 30 min.		37 hr.	3 hr.	10 hr. 30 min.
# WORKERS	1	1-3	1-3		
MISC. WORK	Soil slip was painted on cement joints	Excavation	Soil mortur to cover cement joints		
MATERIALS	Thick soil slip	(none)	(Refer to Report 33)		
TIME	30 min	19 hr.			
TOTAL TIME	28 hr.	19 hr.	37 hr.	3 hr.	10 hr. 30 min.

AREA	KIVA B	ROOM 27	KIVA B	KIVA B	ROOM 31
TYPE OF JOB	Excavation of 10-20cm above floor and cleaning	Permanent Roof	Permanent Roof	Drainage method for roof	Steps built into room 31.
# WORKERS		1	2		
CEMENT					
SAND		8	14		
CEMENT		2 2/3	4 2/3		
TIME		3 hr.	1 hr.		
# WORKERS	1-4	2	1-6	2-3	2
MISC. WORK	Removal of soil	Chiseling sockets in wall & building roof	Construction of roof	Excavation. Drain pipe insertion.	Steps built of left over beam sections.
MATERIALS	(none)	3 Beams: 1 - 8'x6" 1 - 8'x9" 1 - 8'x11" 2 sheets of plywood; ½ roll of tar-paper; 1 cu. yd. of soil	(Refer to description)	8-10' Sections of plastic. 4" sewer pipe; 1 - 45° coupling 1 - Roll 4x15 F15 insulation; wire screen 4 - 1' sec. 2x4	3 - 3' sections of beam
TIME	49 hr.	12 hr.	145 hr.	32 hr.	2 hr.
TOTAL TIME	49 hr.	27 hr.	143 hr.	32 hr.	4 hr.

www.ingramcontent.com/pod-product-compliance
Lightning Source LLC
Chambersburg PA
CBHW051958280526
45793CB00005B/769